Mastery

of

Abundant

Living

Christian Keys
to the
Law of Attraction

Bruce Goldwell
Tammy Lynch
Deborah M. Buchanan

With Excerpt by Carmen J. Day

ISBN 978-1-897512-01-2
Copyright © Bruce Goldwell 2007
Bruce Goldwell
Cover ꭱꞇ
Saga Books
www.Sagabooks.net

FORWARD

There are thousands of religions in the world with people believing in God and his Universe in so many different ways and each having a different understanding and/or belief in what our role as living beings among that creation is or should be. The view points expressed in this book are from the perspective of what those of the Christian faith derive their belief system from which is the ancient writings of the Bible. The scriptures contained herein are used to support the various ideas and feelings shared by the authors and it is up to the individual reader to reflect upon of all of this and come to their own conclusion.

I am honored by my esteemed co-authors of *Mastery of Abundant Living* and pleased with the contributions they have made to this book. Their willingness to share their thoughts, feelings and wisdom in creating this book is a blessing. It is my great pleasure to thank them for their contribution. I am sure that readers of this book will understand how their writings have helped so much to add to the impact of its contents.

God's laws are *Universal*. The *Laws of Attraction, Abundance, Love* and all other laws are *Universal* laws. By understanding how these laws relate to Christian values and beliefs, believers can have more wealth, health and love in their life and have these things in great abundance. We invite you to read this work and pray about the information we have shared. God's blessing will be upon all those who understand and follow in the path of righteousness and love.

Namaste

THE SECOND EPISTLE GENERAL OF

PETER

CHAPTER 1: 5-8

"And beside this, giving all diligence, add to your faith virtue; and to virtue knowledge;

And to knowledge temperance; and to temperance patience; and to patience godliness;

And to godliness brotherly kindness; and to brotherly kindness charity.

For if these things be in you, and abound, they make you that ye shall neither be barren nor unfruitful in the knowledge of our Lord Jesus Christ."

Christian Keys to the Law of Attraction

Bruce Goldwell

Accepting Abundance as God's Gift

"Consider this: whoever sows sparingly will also reap sparingly, and whoever sows bountifully will also reap bountifully. Each must do as already determined, without sadness or compulsion, for God loves a cheerful giver. Moreover, God is able to make every grace abundant for you, so that in all things, always having all you need, you may have abundance for every good work. "

2 Corinthians 9

The first idea we will explore, which is the beginning of your journey in attaining the "*Mastery of Abundant Living,*" is that you live in a Universe that is filled with abundance, and that God provides sufficiency in everything.

God created an abundant Universe and a world that man can live upon that is also abundant. One of his first instructions to mankind was to live in abundance. Genesis 9:7: "... *be ye fruitful, and multiply; bring forth abundantly in the earth, and multiply therein."*

When you consider that God is everywhere and permeates everything, there is no surprise that everything is in abundance in the Universe. If God is within us and we individually are part of the Universe, why do you think that some live in abundance and others do not? It's simply because they have chosen it that way. That's correct. Our *free will* has allowed us to decide that this is the way it is.

> *"Look at the birds in the sky; they do not sow or reap, they gather nothing into barns, yet your heavenly Father feeds them. Are not you more important than they? Can any of you by worrying add a single moment to your life-span?"*

There is no lack upon this earth. There is abundance in all things. God created it to be so. The birds of the air have plenty for their needs. It is the same with man. There is plenty for all. However because people are lead to believe that there is some kind of lack in this world, they are lead to live in lack and not partake of the wonderful blessings that this life has to offer. Joy and peace are replaced with worry and grief and those that live in this condition become the victims of their own beliefs.

When you give abundantly, abundance is part of your life. When you give sparingly, then there is lack in your life. You must choose if you are going to live in abundance or live in lack and that is a matter of *belief and faith.*

"*To him who hath will be given more but to him who hath not will be taken away even that which he hath.*" We live in a world where the rich keep getting richer and the poor keep getting poorer. This is not by some act of man, accident, or some government default that this occurs. You are rewarded with more abundance when you are living the law of abundance and you repel abundance when you avoid being abundant yourself.

"*Why are you anxious about clothes? Learn from the way the wild flowers grow. They do not work or spin. But I tell you that not even Solomon in all his splendor was clothed like one of them. If God so clothes the grass of the field, which grows today and is thrown into the oven tomorrow, will he not much more provide for you, O you of little faith?*"

"*So do not worry and say, 'What are we to eat?' or 'What are we to drink?' or 'What are we to wear?' All these things the pagans seek. Your heavenly Father knows that you need them all. But seek first the kingdom (of God) and his righteousness, and all these things will be given you besides.*"

Matthew 6:26-33

God did not intend for man to worry over such things as where was his food going to come from and how was he to provide for his family, all that exist upon this earth is for mans use. Yet so many people give up their inherent right to share in the rich blessings of this life to live a life that is lacking and needy. This is simply a choice that one makes and not one that is forced upon them.

By first recognizing that the Universe is abundant, that you live in a world that is abundant, and that your life can be one of abundance in health, wealth and love, you can then begin to create a life for you and your family that is filled and your cup will overflow.

Let's consider a few more scriptures on the idea of abundance:

> "And to know the love of Christ, which passeth knowledge, that ye might be filled with all the fullness of God. Now unto him that is able to do exceeding abundantly above all that we ask or think, according to the power that worketh in us, unto him be glory..."
> Ephesians 3:20

> "And the children of Israel were faithful and increased abundantly, and multiplied, and waxed exceeding mighty; and the land was filled with them."
> Ex: 1:7

"Therefore the LORD established the kingdom in his hand; and all Judah brought to Jehoshaphat presents; and he had riches and honour in abundance."

2 Chr. 17:5

It was not God's intention for man to live in poverty. God rejoices in man enjoying the fruits of this earth. It is not for any of us to envy those who live in abundance. To do so is to go against the very nature of what God truly wants of us. Those that envy others for their wealth will by virtue of the Law of Attraction repel the very thing that they envy. To attract abundance into our life, we must be thankful for what we have and rejoice for those what we see who are basking in the fruits of God's blessings. In doing this, we begin to attract into our life the very thing that we thank him for blessing others with.

To enter into the realm of abundance in health, wealth and love we must be appreciative in the fact that God has given us a world filled with abundance and be open to receiving such into our life. By doing this, we begin to live the Law of Attraction in such a way that we actually magnetize the abundance into our life. We will attract opportunity, the right people and the right circumstances that will continually lead us to even more abundance. *"To him who hath will be given more..."*

9

THOUGHTS

The God Consciousness

"...Do you not know that your body is a temple of the Holy Spirit who is in you, whom you have from God, and that you are not your own?"

1 Corinthians 6:19-20

God is within you! Here in lies the "SECRET" of the *"Mastery of Abundant Living"*...the One Spirit within each of us is All Powerful, has unlimited resources and has everything in abundance. This simple understanding is essential to most that have learned to master abundant living.

> *"I, then, a prisoner for the Lord, urge you to live in a manner worthy of the call you have received, with all humility and gentleness, with patience, bearing with one another through love, striving to preserve the unity of the spirit through the bond of peace: one body and one Spirit, as you were also called to the one hope of your call; one Lord, one faith, one baptism; one God and Father of all, who is over all and through all and in all."*

We are all united in Him! *"Know ye not that ye are the temple of the living God?"* There are many times the Bible makes reference to God being within you. *"I AM the Shepherd."* "I and my Father are One." And so on...

"There are different kinds of spiritual gifts but the same Spirit; there are different forms of service but the same Lord; there are different workings but the same God who produces all of them in everyone. To each individual the manifestation of the Spirit is given for some benefit. To one is given through the Spirit the expression of wisdom; to another the expression of knowledge according to the same Spirit; to another faith by the same Spirit; to another gifts of healing by the one Spirit; to another mighty deeds; to another prophecy; to another discernment of spirits; to another varieties of tongues; to another interpretation of tongues. But one and the same Spirit produces all of these, distributing them individually to each person as he wishes."

1 Corinthians 12:4-11

"To each individual the manifestation of the Spirit is given for some benefit." The One Spirit that is within each of us is the core of our being. This is not difficult for most to understand. Now relate God's unlimited power and resources to this belief. Can you believe that God has all of the resources in abundance and is willing to guide us to that in which we ask for?

So if God is within us and there is no question that He has everything ever needed to guide the circumstances we desire to us, then why is it then that sometimes we have things that appear in our lives that are not what we desire? We think, "I didn't ask for that. I wanted something completely different." The difficulty has been as simple as how we ask - our faith and beliefs.

Unfortunately, most of us have not been taught or how to ask for what we desire. Most don't really understand how to allow God's *Unlimited Power* within us to work to the benefit of all as well as ourselves, and therefore, we don't receive what we want. We receive what we focus upon.

For example, many people who want to become healthier and decide that they want to lose weight constantly think and speak about food, and how much over weight they are. They want to be thinner, but they focus upon how heavy they are. They intend to diet really hard, and sacrifice. They compromise by eating what they don't like, and doing dreadful exercises. They know it will be difficult to become the weight they desire, and realistically, they don't ever expect to achieve it, but they'll give it their best shot.

Unfortunately, they expect exactly what they get and what they'll continue to get as long as they expect it. Where is the faith in that? We have to change our thinking from wishing and hoping to intending and expecting. Faith in knowing it will be delivered is the difference. There is no place for doubtful thinking. There is no place for doubting that what you seek in prayer will be delivered.

"Consider it all joy, my brothers, when you

encounter various trials, for you know that the testing of your faith produces perseverance. And let perseverance be perfect, so that you may be perfect and complete, lacking in nothing.

'But if any of you lacks wisdom, he should ask God who gives to all generously and ungrudgingly, and he will be given it. But he should ask in faith, not doubting, for the one who doubts is like a wave of the sea that is driven and tossed about by the wind. For that person must not suppose that he will receive anything from the Lord, since he is a man of two minds, unstable in all his ways."

James 1:2-8

Money and time are two things most believe they don't have enough of, wouldn't you agree? When you say you don't have the money for this or the time for that, you set yourself up for never having the money or time. Even if you are thinking or saying, "I wish I had the money to travel to some foreign place or take a cruise", you are focusing upon the fact that you now don't have enough. If you are constantly talking and thinking about not enough, and begging in prayer you will likely never have enough.

Wishing is just that! It is a future hope, and as long as it is a future hope in your mind, it will remain a future hope in your reality. To realize your true desires, you must have faith. You must be

14

constantly thinking and speaking with the expectation of your desires materializing in order to cause its manifestation. You have to "*reprogram*" yourself to expect to attain that which you desire.

When you look up "want" versus "expect" in the dictionary, you get very different meanings.

Want: desire, wish for, fancy, crave, yearn for.

Expect: wait for, anticipate, look forward to, count on, demand, insist on.

Think of the difference between a married couple who wants to have children, and a married couple who is expecting. How do they think about their future and how do they act? Your thoughts and actions about what you desire must be that distinctively different so that you expect what you desire.

"I plan to travel to some foreign place or take a cruise." This is a much better thought than, "I wish I had the money to travel to some foreign place or take a cruise." The first way of expressing your desire shows your expectation of attaining your desire. Better yet, if you begin to gather the information about your trip, start planning what you'll do, and continue to say to yourself that somehow, some way, you know it will happen. Then the Power of Prayer, or also commonly referred to as the law of attraction will set the forces in motion through God's unlimited resources of the One Spirit in which you are united, and the events that need to occur to deliver to you the circumstance of your true intent will manifest.

In order to change from wishful thinking that gets undesirable results, to manifestation or anticipative thinking, which brings about your true desires, you have to change the way you think and speak on an every day basis. You must have faith and know that what it is you desire will be delivered. This is how you pray correctly. This is what faith is all about.

> "...he should ask in faith, not doubting, for the one who doubts is like a wave of the sea that is driven and tossed about by the wind. For that person must not suppose that he will receive anything from the Lord..."

> James 1:6-7

It's about faith. Know that your prayers are answered every time in accordance with that in which you believe, in accordance with whom you become in consciousness.

Though you might not currently have the money or resources to achieve something you want to do, you can always speak and think in a way that attracts the money and resources to you. When you start to live life this way, everything you desire comes to you, and you are living the true nature of the law of attraction, and you have learned to true Power of Prayer.

Now there is good news and bad news. The good

news is that you already have access to this power and access to all of God's unlimited resources and you are already a master at using the law of attraction, and every prayer is answered every time.

You can change your life right now by deciding to consciously direct the outcome of the *Power of Prayer*, instead of allowing your thoughts to be your prayer without your conscious direction. Your past does not determine your future. However, it is your present thoughts and desires that will. Again, it is not your past that determines your future; it is your current thoughts and prayers that determine your future.

Everything that manifests in your life is based on the *Power of Prayer* and living God's Will. If you are thinking poor and acting in a manor in which you are not giving, you are attracting poverty and lack.

A lady once decided she was not going to tip as much when she went to restaurants. She began being tight with her money and not being as giving in her donations to charity, church and other things. It was only a short time and she found that she was having less money herself to work with. Her decision to give less began creating lack in her own life.

If you are thinking abundantly and acting abundantly by giving of yourself in abundance, then you are attracting abundance and wealth.

Many people find that when they begin to give to

charities that for some reason more money begins to show up in their life. The same is true for those who exercise faith and begin to tithe in their church. God always promises that when you give a portion of your abundance to help build his kingdom He will pour out more abundance into the givers life. The stories about this are endless and yet many people will still refuse to give up any thing that comes into their life. Who does it all belong to anyhow? The wealthy hotel tycoon by the name of Marriott once said, "*This is not my money, I am just the custodian of it.*" Marriott understood that the riches he was given didn't really belong to him, he was just to administer it righteously.

In order to change your world, you first have to change your thoughts, prayers and beliefs. If you will change, everything will change for you.

> *"Do to others whatever you would have them do to you. This is the law and the prophets."*

Matthew 7:6

You Outer World is a mirror reflection of your Inner World. Your actions are determined by your beliefs and your beliefs are shaped by your predominant thoughts.

Thought is the seed of reality! Remember that God is listening all the time and the words that you say to yourself is also prayer, whether you intend it or not. Thought is what ultimately controls your destiny. When you control your thoughts, you shape your expectations and the realities of your expectations are delivered to you through the *Natural Laws* of God.

Whether your thoughts are consciously being controlled to focus upon the expectation of that which you desire, or not, your thoughts will control your destiny every time. So the question is, do you want to control your destiny or not?

If you are not controlling your thoughts, you are not controlling your destiny and when you arrive at a destination, it will likely not be what you want it to be. However, whether you want it or not, your destination is always without fail a result of previous thoughts that you created and nourished. It's the result of what you convinced yourself to believe. It's the result of exactly what your faith guides you to.

> *"When he was going back to the city in the morning, he was hungry. Seeing a fig tree by the road, he went over to it, but found nothing on it except leaves. And he said to it, 'May no fruit ever come from you again.' And immediately the fig tree withered. When the disciples saw this, they were amazed and said, 'How was it that the fig tree withered immediately?' Jesus said to them in reply, 'Amen, I say to you, if you have faith and do not waver, not only will you do what has been done to the fig tree, but even if you say to this mountain, 'Be lifted up and thrown*

into the sea,' it will be done. Whatever you ask for in prayer with faith, you will receive.'"

Matthew 21:18-22

The words you say to yourself in silence, your predominant thoughts are prayers. Prayer in faith is how you attain mastery over every outer world circumstance.

You can control all things in the outer world through faith in the *Power of Prayer*. All things that come into your life are a result of the thoughts you focus your attention upon. Focusing only on thoughts of what you truly long for, emotionally, psychologically, intellectually and spiritually, with the expectation of success and to the benefit of all and you will cause those thoughts to become your reality.

How Do Negative Thoughts Affect Our Lives?

> *"Let love be sincere; hate what is evil, hold on to what is good; love one another with mutual affection; anticipate one another in showing honor. Do not grow slack in zeal, be fervent in spirit, serve the Lord. Rejoice in hope, endure in affliction, and persevere in prayer. Contribute to the needs of the holy ones, exercise hospitality. Bless those who persecute (you), bless and do not curse them. Rejoice with those who rejoice, weep*

with those who weep. Have the same regard for one another; do not be haughty but associate with the lowly; do not be wise in your own estimation. Do not repay anyone evil for evil; be concerned for what is noble in the sight of all. If possible, on your part, live at peace with all. Beloved, do not look for revenge but leave room for the wrath; for it is written, 'Vengeance is mine, I will repay, says the Lord.' Rather, 'if your enemy is hungry, feed him; if he is thirsty, give him something to drink; for by so doing you will heap burning coals upon his head.' Do not be conquered by evil but conquer evil with good."

Romans 12:9-21

You cannot change what has happened in your past; you can only change how you think about it and how you think about the future. How you have thought in the past has landed you where we are today. The awesome aspect of all of this is that you can control what is to be our destiny regardless of our past and you do that by starting today with our thoughts. Silent thoughts are heard by God as prayer. Your today thoughts shape your expectations and what you become and therefore what you will be delivered in the future. If you want a destiny of abundance, prosperity and love, you begin by starting this very moment to nurture only those thoughts that will bring about the manifestation of those desires.

Complaining about your status in life, your relationship with others or any circumstance will only serve to continue its existence. Only by deciding to start from this moment on with thoughts about how your life is transformed and that everything you are attracting into your life are things that create more abundance, love and prosperity will you begin living an abundant life. Your prayerful thoughts must be consistent with Romans 12:9-21.

"Ascending in consciousness to that which you desire to be, this is the way you attract an outer world consistent with your desires. Jesus said, *"I AM the way."* His awareness of being is the way. Follow Jesus' example. Get the consciousness of who you desire to become and the things in your outer world are compelled to appear through God's Omnipotent Power."

You are told to "*Seek ye first the kingdom of Heaven and all things shall be added unto you.*" Become what you desire in consciousness first, paying no attention to the outer world. This is the meaning of "*Ye shall decree a thing and it shall come to pass.*"

Start right now to live the *Law of Attraction* through the *Power of Prayer* with thoughts of drawing abundance, love and prosperity unto all and you will soon see the manifestation of such as your destiny unfolds. It will be no surprise to you when you get there because it will be exactly what you expect, nothing more and nothing less. You will become a magnet for everything you desire in life when you ascend in consciousness and your thoughts begin to bring forth feelings in you that create expectations, which will eventually manifest the reality of those things upon which you focused your thoughts.

Your prayerful thought of what you desire eventually become subconscious expectations and these empowering expectations will cause the manifestation of your desire every time.

"*Sew a thought, reap an act.*" For every thought there is a corresponding manifestation. For every action, there's a reaction. Thought is the action that starts the chain of events that leads to the corresponding manifestation, which is the reaction. Thought is the cause, and your reality is the effect. When you learn to control your thoughts to only those in accordance with the Will of God, you will be able to have things that manifest into your life that are in line with your true desires.

THOUGHTS

_____

_____

_____

_____

_____

_____

_____

_____

_____

_____

Universal Laws are God's Laws

"Do not be deceived, God is not mocked; for whatever a man sows, this he will also reap. For the one who sows to his own flesh will from the flesh reap corruption, but the one who sows to the Spirit will from the Spirit reap eternal life. Let us not lose heart in doing good, for in due time we will reap if we do not grow weary. So then, while we have opportunity, let us do good to all people, and especially to those who are of the household of the faith. "

Galatians 6

There are Laws that the Universe responds to every time. The Laws below are a few that make the *Power of Prayer* and the *Law of Attraction* work.

- Law of Vibration

- Law of Love

- Law of Fair Exchange

- Law of Growth

Let's start with the *Law of Vibration*, as this is an important principle in how the *Power of Prayer* works. Everything has a vibration. Vibration attracts like vibrations. When a certain key is hit on a piano it will make a crystal chandelier shake. The crystals in the chandelier have a vibration and the correct key on a piano that is in concert with that vibration makes the crystal shake. You want to be vibrating in harmony with those things you want to attract into your life.

For example, you can't attract the perfect companion if you are not the perfect companion for them. You both have to be vibrating at the same frequency. You can't attract prosperity and abundance if you are not in harmony with their vibrations either. It is our feelings that tell us if we are vibrationally aligned. If you have feelings on un-easiness you are not vibrationally aligned. It is God giving you the direction.

By nurturing thoughts of prosperity for everyone, which eventually will start to create feelings inside of you that are in harmony with prosperity, you will begin to attract all things prosperous into your life. Just like the *Law of Gravity*, if you fall, you will fall toward the earth, with the law of vibration when you are in the right vibration, you will attract a like vibration. Thus your outer world is determined by your inner world. You control your thoughts therefore you control your destiny.

Your destiny can now be one of prosperity, love and abundance because you now know the true essence of the *Power of Prayer*. Start today by nurturing thoughts of prosperity, love and abundance and the day will soon come that the manifestation of such will become your reality.

We are *One Body* and as a part of the *Body of Christ*, we cannot provoke or alienate any other part of the Body and gain personal benefit. Meaning, we cannot harm others and gain long term. As *One Body*, the happiness, peace and harmony within the Universe depend upon the individual recognizing the interests of each of its members. So everything you think and do affects everyone and everything in the Universe. Everything is felt throughout the Universe to some degree, yet you will never personally benefit as a result of imposing harm to any part of the *One Body*. If you harm others, you harm the *Body of Christ* and as part of the *Body*, you harm yourself.

Conversely, if you do great things for others, you improve the *One Body* and as part of the *Body* you will benefit.

> "*As a body is one though it has many parts, and all the parts of the body, though many, are one body, so also Christ. For in one Spirit we were all baptized into one body, whether Jews or Greeks, slaves or free persons, and we were all given to drink of one Spirit. Now the body is not a single part, but many. If a foot should say, "Because I am not a hand I do not belong to the body," it does not for this reason belong any less to the body. Or if an ear should say, "Because I am not an eye I do not belong to the body," it does not for this reason belong any less to the body. If the whole body were an eye, where would the hearing be? If the whole body were hearing, where would the sense of smell be? But as it is, God placed the parts, each one of them, in*

the body as he intended. If they were all one part, where would the body be? But as it is, there are many parts, yet one body. The eye cannot say to the hand, "I do not need you," nor again the head to the feet, "I do not need you." Indeed, the parts of the body that seem to be weaker are all the more necessary, and those parts of the body that we consider less honorable we surround with greater honor, and our less presentable parts are treated with greater propriety, whereas our more presentable parts do not need this. But God has so constructed the body as to give greater honor to a part that is without it, so that there may be no division in the body, but that the parts may have the same concern for one another. If (one) part suffers, all the parts suffer with it; if one part is honored, all the parts share its joy.

Now you are Christ's body, and individually parts of it. Some people God has designated in the church to be, first, apostles; second, prophets; third, teachers; then, mighty deeds; then, gifts of healing, assistance, administration, and varieties of tongues. Are all apostles? Are all prophets? Are all teachers? Do all work mighty deeds? Do all have gifts of healing? Do all speak in tongues? Do all interpret? Strive eagerly for the greatest spiritual gifts. But I shall show you a still more excellent way."

1 Corinthians 12

Another principle or Law is the *Law of Reciprocity*. The *One Body* will return to you that which you deliver to the *Body*. With every thought, if you keep this in mind, you will change your thoughts to be constructive and you will not waste time or money on things that don't work within this principle. Many consider this the law of love. If you have unconditional love for everyone, you will give accordingly and therefore reap unconditional love in exchange.

> "*If I speak with the tongues of men and of angels, but do not have love, I have become a noisy gong or a clanging cymbal. If I have the gift of prophecy, and know all mysteries and all knowledge; and if I have all faith, so as to remove mountains, but do not have love, I am nothing. And if I give all my possessions to feed the poor, and if I surrender my body to be burned, but do not have love, it profits me nothing.*
>
> "*Love is patient, love is kind and is not jealous; love does not brag and is not arrogant, does not act unbecomingly; it does not seek its own, is not provoked, does not take into account a wrong suffered, does not rejoice in unrighteousness, but rejoices with the truth; bears all things, believes all things, hopes all things, endures all things.*
>
> "*Love never fails; but if there are gifts of prophecy, they will be done away; if there are tongues, they will cease; if there is*

knowledge, it will be done away.

1 Corinthians 13

The *Law of Love* means you are to hate nothing.

The *Law of Fair Exchange* says that your result will be in direct proportion to your effort. Living your life under God's Will and the *Law of Love* becomes a habit by practice. Repetition is the mother of skill. If you aren't already a master of correct, constructive thinking, now is the time to teach yourself. You will benefit from learning and integrating this principle in direct proportion to the effort you extend in learning it right now.

Here's where you can start.

- I <u>can be</u> what I decide to be.

- I <u>can be</u> what I desire to be.

- I <u>can be</u> what I will to be.

Begin repeating these vision statements (affirmations) every morning and every night and multiple times throughout the day until it becomes a belief, while keeping in mind who and what the "I" really is. The spiritual "I" that understands that you cannot harm any other part of the *One Body* in which we are all united and benefit in any way.

Eventually, through repetition, this practice creates a new habit. Doing or saying something over and over until your subconscious has accepted it as a belief that you instinctively act upon creates habits. "*Sow a thought, reap and act, sow and act, reap a habit.*"

You will begin to believe these statements and this belief will be instinctively acted upon. When you instinctively act upon these statements of belief, you will unconsciously begin praying correctly and through the *Power of Prayer* and the Omnipotence of God within, you will become invincible.

Ensure that instead of living your life based on the habit of failure, that you create a new habit of success, which is a requirement to living in abundance. What is the success habit? It is quite simple... do what you say you're going to do. Starting something with no intention of finishing it creates a habit of failure. Think about it. If you set goals that are achievable, and you simply don't follow through three out of four times, then you have created a belief that you fail at whatever you decide to accomplish. This is extremely dis-empowering. Jim Rohn, a business philosopher says, "*Something that is easy to do, is also easy not to do.*" Don't get into the habit of not completing your easy predetermined goals even if it's easy to do. You create the habit of failure, instead of the habit of success.

When you decide, you must follow through because it is the lack of following through that creates the habit of failure. If this has been your past, change it today. Decide today you are going to repeat these vision statements mornings, evening, and several times throughout the day. Maybe at first you only want to commit to doing this for two weeks. Then after you've been successful accomplishing this two-week goal, and then extend it two more weeks, and so on.

Once you have completed your commitment to yourself, you will have planted a seed of an empowering belief about your ability to be what you desire at will. You will also have created a success habit that will be so deep within your subconscious that when your goal is much larger, your subconscious will just kick in and execute based on your new habit of success.

Ultimately, do not say you'll "*try*" to do anything that you are capable of doing unless you are committed to following it through. Again, the words to use when undertaking any new endeavor or task is to say, "I *will* do it."

The first thing you must do in order to serve others is to make sure you have the wherewithal to do so. You cannot be generous to others unless you have nothing to give. You cannot give and serve others, unless you are strong. You have access and the right to all of the abundance in the Universe in order to be strong to serve others. You have access to all of the abundance and as long as you live within the God's Law of love, what you desire is within your command and will be delivered.

God expresses and creates through the individual, and the individual expresses through the *One Body* that unites us. When you live by God's *Will* and all that is good, and is of service to others, the *One Spirit* in which we are all united sets the forces in motion so that evidence of your faith is delivered. Seek inspiration, and become one with the *Holy Spirit* within you. It is your realization and acknowledgement that God is within you that will allow you access to life's abundance.

Your Spirit is the part of you that is united with the *Holy Spirit*, the *One Spirit* in which we are all united. It is the part of you that is the Creator within your conscious influence. It is most important for you to come into realization of your conscious power, the power of prayer in faith, the power that comes from ascending in consciousness to that which you desire.

Your conscious thoughts create your habits and beliefs. It creates your awareness of who you are, or your awareness of being. So it is crucial for you to understand your conscious power.

Power comes through tranquility... seek silence and stillness often because if you quite your mind and body, you can think correctly and it is prayerful thought that is the secret to creativity and ultimately your ability to manifest your desires.

The *Law of Vibration* carries light and electricity. We know it works, even though we don't see it. Thought, similarly, is carried through the *Law of Vibration.* So thought vibrates beyond our physical being and unites with God. All thought is a form of prayer. God listens to all of our thoughts, not just those we call prayer. A realization that all thought is prayer will change the way you think.

Now consider the *Law of Love*. Love is God's *Will*, so thoughts based in Love are given vitality. It's the *Law of Growth* in which thoughts take form and expression. It is your emotions that give feeling to thoughts so that thoughts will take form. If you have a thought that is based upon the law of love, it consistent with God's *Will* takes form through the Law of Growth.

How do we develop the faith, courage and passion, which will accomplish this chain of events that will ultimately deliver to you the expression of your thoughts and desires? Practice and repetition! Not the practice of negative behaviors, but rather the practice of perfect prayers, correct thought. "*Perfect practice makes perfect*". When we practice perfect principles based on the God's *Universal Laws*, the manifestations of those perfect practices are always in line with what we desire.

Many people think about acquiring things for selfish reasons. The more you think about serving others, and you realize that selfish thoughts are the poison that will kill any positive growth, the more you will come to know the true power of your thoughts. The more we serve, the more we will receive. "*Sow abundance, reap abundance*!"

"*I am the true vine, and My Father is the vinedresser. Every branch in Me that does not*

34

bear fruit, He takes away; and every branch that bears fruit, He prunes it so that it may bear more fruit. Abide in Me, and I in you. As the branch cannot bear fruit of itself unless it abides in the vine, so neither can you unless you abide in Me."

John 15:5

THOUGHTS

Becoming Fearless Like Christ

"*Let love be without hypocrisy. Abhor what is evil; cling to what is good. Be devoted to one another in brotherly love; give preference to one another in honor; not lagging behind in diligence, fervent in spirit, serving the Lord; rejoicing in hope, persevering in tribulation, devoted to prayer, contributing to the needs of the saints, practicing hospitality. Bless those who persecute you; bless and do not curse. Rejoice with those who rejoice, and weep with those who weep. Be of the same mind toward one another; do not be haughty in mind, but associate with the lowly. Do not be wise in your own estimation. Never pay back evil for evil to anyone. Respect what is right in the sight of all men. If possible, so far as it depends on you, be at peace with all men...*"

The *Power of Prayer* will draw to you that which is most predominant in our mind. If your predominant thought is constructive and harmonious, your result will be constructive; if your thought is destructive or discordant, your result will be destructive. This could possibly be the origin of good and evil. Good, being that of love for all, and fear being our personal devil. Fear can be hate, guilt, worry, anxiety, or many other emotions that don't feel very good and ultimately relate back to some form of fear.

Fear will always take us away from the things we want and love and faith will always take us toward the things we want. The *Law of Vibration* simply will not let two conflicting ideas come together. If you desire something yet fear aspects of what that desire entails, you will simply be keeping your desire away from you.

Initially couples meet, find common ground from which they can build a relationship, fall in love, get married, and begin raising a family. Some relationship last a lifetime. Others begin to fall apart somewhere along the line and end in divorce. The *Law of Attraction* works every time without fail. The *Law of Attraction* brings to people together and the *Law of Attraction* can also separate people even if at one time they were a happy loving couple.

Keep in mind that love will always take us toward those things we want and fear will always take us away from the things we want. Once fear enters into a relationship, it is only a matter of time before that relationship will end.

Couples who are suffering and find their marriage falling apart would do well to sit down and express their feelings and what fears they might be experiencing. Fear is the root of all evil. When something is amiss, fear is most likely at the root of it. Get rid of the fear and allow love to be the predominate factor in the relationship and couples will again be moving toward the things they want.

Prayer is an important part of any relationship. We give thanks for the things we want in life, we ask God for the things we hope to have in the near future, and we look forward with faith for the manifestation of those prayers. If we are praying for a marriage that is not working and has gone amiss, we should also work toward solutions based on the inspired thoughts that God sends to us. *"Faith without works is dead being alone."* If you are praying for healing in a relationships you must be part of that healing process which also means speaking with your spouse or significant other to find out what is at the core of it.

Christ is the author of love. When asking people on the street if they thought Christ was afraid of anything the answer has always been a resounding "no". We can renew our life, relationships and all facets of our life by becoming like Christ by becoming fearless. In the "Mastery of Abundant Living" The Key to Mastering the Law of Attraction, the questions and solutions for overcoming fear were shared with readers. By working as best you can to overcome the one attitude which is the basis for so many negative emotions and with the *Power of Prayer* and God's help, one can rid their life of this root of all evil.

> "*So I declare and testify in the Lord that you must no longer live as the Gentiles do, in the futility of their minds; darkened in understanding, alienated from the life of God because of their ignorance, because of their hardness of heart, they have become callous and have handed themselves over to licentiousness for the practice of every kind of impurity to excess. That is not how you learned Christ, assuming that you have heard of him and were taught in him, as truth is in Jesus, that you should put away the old self of your former way of life, corrupted through deceitful desires, and be renewed in the spirit of your minds, and put on the new self,*

created in God's way in righteousness and holiness of truth."

Ephesians 4:17-24

In order to change the "*world-without*" we must change the "*world-within*". You "should put away the old self" and ascend in consciousness to that which you want to be. God is with you. The power of the *Body of Christ* and the *Holy Spirit* which unites everyone is with you and permeates everything.

There is nothing in your outer world that can harm you when you have faith. By getting rid of fear from your inner world, you immediately change your outer world and begin to experience those things that come to those who vibrate in the realm of love. The kind of friends that you make will be more loving, the relationships you have will be more loving, and all business and personal relationships will be those whose vibrations are love. You will be able to tell the difference between the two. You will instinctively stay away from those people who are not conducive to the new vibration you are living.

Everyone seems to seek three basic things in life: Health, Wealth and Love. Of these three, love is the one thing that affects all other things in our lives. When we don't feel love, we can suffer poor health and it might even affect our performance at work, which can affect the incomes we receive. It also affects our ability to have trusting relationships, which will affect our ability to earn, because in all financial ventures trusting relationships are crucial.

When we increase the love in our life, all other things can also increase as well as our health and our abundance.

We feel love in two ways: Love from others and love of self. By first loving yourself, we open up the door to feel more love from others. By loving yourself, you also have the capacity to love others more. Getting rid of fear allows us to love our self as well as others more abundantly.

A few scriptures that support releasing fear:

> *"I sought the LORD, and he heard me, and delivered me from all my fears."*
>
> PS. 34:4

> "But even the very hairs of your head are all numbered. Fear not therefore: ye are of more value than many sparrows."
>
> Luke. 12:7

> *"There is no fear in love; but perfect love casteth out fear: because fear hath torment. He that feareth is not made perfect in love."*
>
> 1 John 4:18

In order to be perfected in Christ, we much be

perfected in our Body and Mind. Releasing fear allows us to live with the inspiration of the *Holy Spirit* and receive inspiration, revelation and live in harmony with all that is Christ driven.

To live in fear is to live contrary to what God wants for us.

> "*For, when we were come into Macedonia, our flesh had no rest, but we were troubled on every side; without were fightings, within were fears.*"
>
> 2 Cor. 7:5

In the '*Mastery of Abundant Living*' one releases the fear which creates the fightings without. The world without is governed by the world within and when there is fear within that will be fightings without. You outside world is truly a reflection of what is going on inside you. When you learn to have peace inside you will have peace without.

The really wonderful thing about the Law of Attraction and all of God's laws is that they are instantaneous. The moment you put the Laws into action that is the very moment that your life is transformed. You can be renewed in Christ by renewing your spirit within. Everything around you will be transformed because you are the one that transformed them. It is a gift from God. The power is within you to do much good. You can begin to exercise that power this very moment.

THOUGHTS

The Substance of Things Hoped For

"Rejoice in the Lord always. I shall say it again: rejoice! Your kindness should be known to all. The Lord is near. Have no anxiety at all, but in everything, by prayer and petition, with thanksgiving, make your requests known to God. Then the peace of God that surpasses all understanding will guard your hearts and minds in Christ Jesus.

"Finally, brothers, whatever is true, whatever is honorable, whatever is just, whatever is pure, whatever is lovely, whatever is gracious, if there is any excellence and if there is anything worthy of praise, think about these things. Keep on doing what you have learned and received and heard and seen in me. Then the God of peace will be with you."

Philippians 4:4-9

"...think about these things" in your mind, picture truth, honor, what is just and pure, what is lovely and gracious. Focus upon the excellence and what is worth of praise, and then the God of peace will be with you.

The *Power of Prayer* is working at all times in your life whether you are aware of it or not. The principles that comprise the God's Law are easy to understand and use. The more proficient we become with the principles the more we will accelerate the process of the manifestation of those things we desire. Our current reality is a result of past prayerful thoughts and beliefs and our current prayerful thoughts are the seeds upon which our future reality originates. By learning the principles and practicing, we empower ourselves to have more abundance, more wealth, more love and more happiness in our lives.

If there is one principle that's considered to be the most crucial in "M*astering*" the Power of Prayer, it is the ability to imagine creatively in your minds eye. When you can see what you desire in your minds eye with the intensity, clarity and passion that utilizes all of your senses, and that vision is consistent with God's Will its manifestation not only eminent but can be accelerated.

It is that first thought that begins the creative process, it is the nurturing of the thought, through creative visualization, that brings it to reality. "*Sew a thought, reap an act...*" This process works every time without fail. Look at what is being manifest in your life right now. Is everything that is in your life at this very moment what you really want or are the things in your life those things that you most think about and talk about? If the things you are experiencing in your life are things you really don't want rather then the things you really desire, then it is time to examine your daily activities, thoughts and conversations.

If you want to change your life, you have to change your predominant thoughts and prayers. What is really awesome about the *Power of Prayer* is the immediacy in how it reacts to what we are doing, saying, thinking and our actions. By focusing your thoughts of what you desire and speaking and acting consistently with those thoughts, you ensure that the outcome of the creative process is exactly what you desired it to be.

Become in consciousness that which you desire to be. When you claim yourself to be anything, you have given that claim to God, and that which you have become in consciousness will return to you.

What is the science that explains this power and gift given to us by God?

The subconscious mind is extremely powerful. It doesn't "*think*" it just does what it's been taught to do with perfection every time. It is a gift from God as it runs our vital organs and everything else that we do without conscious thought. Additionally, it doesn't know the difference between fiction and reality. So if we train our subconscious by showing it the perfect picture of our desired reality, it will act as if it's true and set the forces in motion through our *One Spirit* to deliver us that which we desire.

Imagine yourself feeling the way you want to feel. Feel the joy and love in your heart, visualize every aspect of your life as you desire it to be in your mind using all the senses to visualize the experience, until you become so absorbed in the experience you become one with it.

Now trust yourself. Your faith in God will be measured by your confidence in yourself. *"No man (manifestation) comes unto me except the Father within me draw him,"* and *"I and my Father are one."* Believe this truth. Have faith in your claim that you vividly imagine until the certainty of your request becomes a belief within you and you become one with it.

At that moment, the Universe will correspond to the nature of your desire and begin manifesting its reality immediately. Everything will come forth in its own due time and always in concert with what is required to bring about the reality of your desire. Using your imagination to begin the creative process of bringing your thoughts into reality is essential to your success.

> *"Imagination is the beginning of creation. You imagine what you desire, you will what you imagine and at last you create what you will."*
>
> George Bernard Shaw

You must have a clear, vivid picture of the desired result as you wish it to be. You must savor in the feelings of enjoying your life this way. You must imagine that you have already achieved it and are now living it. It is when you become it in consciousness that the miraculous power of the *One Body, One Spirit* delivers your desires in the outer world.

Not only does imagining things from this perspective allow you to understand what is to become of your future, but you will develop faith, confidence, endurance, courage and enthusiasm for your desires. You will develop a passion for your desires, and for life. You will develop faith in God and the *Body of Christ*.

So...what are your dreams?

You can begin right now to use the creative process to set in motion the *Power of Prayer* so your dreams will become your future reality. "*If it's to be, it's up to me*." You are the one who controls what your future has in store for you.

It is a simple process and with time, you will become more and more proficient at it. Don't worry if you don't see every detail. What is important is that your thought process allows you to think of as many details as possible. Each time you can build upon the scenario of your dream. The manifestation of what you imagine will always be more exciting when you get there then what you might possibly dream up in your mind yet it will always be in line with what you desired.

Additionally, once you have a vivid picture and can see it clearly in you mind, ask yourself how you got to that point. Replay your perfect mental visualization backwards in your mind. This will help to anchor it the understanding of cause and effect.

It's as if you're creating a video of your perfect reality in reverse while winding the reel so that it can be played out in real life. It shouldn't include every aspect of what will occur in the process, as God has unlimited resources and will better deliver the correct path. He knows better how to fill in the blanks. However, it is nice to have some key elements of what the creative process will unfold so that you recognize the road marks when you get there.

> *"For we are saved by hope: but hope that is seen is not hope: for what a man seeth, why doth he yet hope for?*
>
> *But if <u>we hope for that we see not</u>, then do <u>we with patience wait for it</u>."*

Rom. 8:24, 25

"Faith is the substance of things hoped for..."

Heb. 11:1

In the scripture given in Romans reference was being made on the idea that we are saved by hope. And hope is not something that is seen. Things that are seen are not knowledge because you can see them. Hoping for that which you can not see but that you hope for, are those things that you wait with patience for, "...*then do we with patience wait for it.*" - was not a question, it was a statement. There was no question mark at the end. The people were being told that they *do with patience wait for it.*

Create the vision of those things that you hope for in your mind. While not materialized yet, the things you hope for are the things which you will eventually manifest into your life. This is why it is so important to focus on the things you want not on things you don't want. Focusing on things you don't want will eventually bring those things upon you.

Have fun with this process. This is your chance to let your imagination fly. Maybe that student who you thought was just daydreaming in the classroom is the one who is using something that God intended for all of us to use in our lives, the creative visualization of our future reality. Wouldn't it be nice if in our educational system they taught people how to think and how to create... *how to dream perfect dreams?*

Go ahead! Find a quiet spot at home, outside near water, on a mountain or any place among nature. All these are wonderful places to dream. Wherever you typically consciously pray and let your imagination soar or simply close your eyes on that trip home on the bus from work. What is most important is that you are taking time out each day to dream of what you want and see it in your mind as already existing. The day will soon come when the manifestation of that dream *will* occur.

THOUGHTS

Accepting Abundance as God's Gift

".. with God all things are possible."
Matt. 19:26

Look at your desires, every desire, as the spoken words of God and every desire a promise. Don't condition your desire. Just accept it as it as it comes and give thanks for it to the point that you're grateful for already receiving it, then go about your way in peace with the faith that God will deliver on His promise. Accept your desire as inspirations from God and have faith that it will manifest. Don't worry about how it will, just know that it will.

How can we say that all desires are the spoken word of God? What if you desire to get revenge on another? How is that an inspiration of God?

No one really wants revenge on another. But because we don't believe that the desire to be free from the other exists we interpret the desire as wanting revenge. We misinterpret the gifts and inspired thought we receive from God because we lack faith.

Almost every minute of every day we are presented with options and opportunities. As you accept your desires and have faith in their manifestations, opportunities that will deliver you your desires will start to unfold before you. When these possibilities present themselves, it is up to you to act. Your actions or lack there of, will determine the path you will take.

The *Body of Christ* has infinite resources and therefore, there are multiple ways that your desires can be delivered, and you may be presented with a possibility that is completely different than what you had in mind. Approaching everything with a detachment to a predetermined path keeps you open to recognize possibilities as they are presented.

Try this exercise and don't look ahead!

1. For about ten seconds, look around the room and try to find everything in the room that's red. Then close your eyes for about ten seconds and remember everything you saw that was red. When you open your eyes, go to step two.

2. Now remember everything that was red. Can you see it in your minds eye even thought your eyes are open? Now without looking around in the room, name everything you saw that was green. Can you remember anything?

Chances are you remembered more red things than green things. When you are focused on a predetermined path, you are not as open to seeing other possibilities. Make sure that you aren't so focused on a specific path that you miss a better opportunity.

Additionally, because God has unlimited resources, you may be given multiple opportunities and have to choose. If you make choices based on a consensus of having asked many others what they would do, the choice you make is still your choice and all the responsibility of those choices is yours and yours alone.

So how can you be sure that the path you choose is the right one?

This is where your feelings come into play. When you feel good about a decision then it is highly probable that it is a good choice. But if somewhere in your gut, something doesn't feel right, then it is probably a decision that will take you further away from your desire.

Most often, however, you should follow your inspiration. Making a decision based on what others prefer should not be your first choice, especially when it goes against your intuition.

You don't drive a car down the road allowing others to steer it for you. The same is true with your life. You want to go through life being the person who chooses what you "*will*" do.

Your *Spirit* has all the resources needed to accomplish anything that you want or desire. As your inner voice becomes more in touch with the *One Spirit* you will be more attune to the inspirations that God offers you. Seek the silence and connect with your *Spirit.* God, through your intuition, will lead you to the wisest choice, and then have faith that you have chosen correctly. The more you detach yourself from a predetermined path and "*allow*" your feelings to be the monitor, the easier it is to stay in harmony with God's *Will,* and it is in harmony where your desires will be manifested with absolute precision.

It might take a little bit of soul searching to find the mindset that is needed in order to be prepared for what the Universe is willing to manifest into your life. The "*allowing*" that is required in order to receive any desire must be unambiguous. You cannot want something and not want something. You can't desire something and yet not be sure you are really ready for it.

By "*allowing*" all possibilities to unfold before you and "*allowing*" yourself to be inspired down the right path, you can be led directly and most assuredly to that thing you desire. No one walks through a closed door. Insure that your "*allowing*" is without doubt, without hesitation and without reservations. You must have faith and courage.

When an opportunity is presented and it feels right, then act, act precisely, act immediately and act unequivocally. Be fully prepared to receive that which you desire and know that your Spirit is united with the One Spirit and that nothing, absolutely nothing that you intend, which is good and in harmony with God's Will, will ever fail to be manifest into your life.

An example of how "*intending*" and "*allowing*" works; we share with you a personal story.

"I, Tammy Lynch, am the President of a multimillion dollar residential development and home building division in Sarasota Florida. My company is merging with another large builder, putting my job at risk. All of the upper management and many of the division management have duplicate roles with the two companies, and one of those duplicate roles is mine.

I was advised about two weeks ago that in order to remain with the company I would be required to relocate to Jacksonville, Florida. My immediate reaction was, "I'm sorry, but I'm not moving." Now this places me as a single mother without financial support from any other source jobless.

Yet I am certain that this is meant to be. I'm not quite sure what it is that I'm going to do, but within two weeks I have three opportunities that have been presented. I'm not stressed about the uncertainty because I know that God always delivers to me that which I desire and solutions beyond what it is I could determine on my own.

I'm excited about the transition that's occurring, even though I don't yet know what

I'm transitioning to. I do know that God always rewards those that have faith and live within God's Will. I guarantee you that the opportunity I choose will be something so much greater than that of staying with my company, because everything that happens to me is for my benefit, as long as I allow it to be.

A friend of mine, Kathy Robinson, suggested that I tell this story in one of my books. She said, "How many people would be out of a job in a month and be excited and smiling about it? You really are living in the Joy of the Lord."

As you can see, Tammy is "*allowing*" all possibilities to unfold before her and she accepted her desire of remaining in Sarasota as God's promise that everything would be all right. By being open to "*receiving*", she worked in harmony with God's *Will* and her future is expected to unfolded and became manifest with exact precision to fulfill Tammy's desires.

Tammy has been consciously with prayerful thought focusing upon a change in lifestyle which will allow her to be able to finish the books she desires to write and to speak and coach others in regards to this topic as well as the seminars she conducts about real estate.

The *Power of Prayer* works every time, without fail, guaranteed! There is no doubt that the opportunities being presented to Tammy will result in exactly the lifestyle and career she has been visualizing. It is exactly what she has risen to in consciousness.

"If thou canst believe, all things are possible to him that believeth."

Matt. 9:23

Every time you manifest a dream or desire, you can build bigger and better dreams. There is no limit to what you can do. Dream big! Dream often! Then have faith that and allow all possibilities to unfold before you. Act when you are inspired and know that you are being led down the right path. The *Kingdom of Heaven* on Earth is within your grasp and the *Body of Christ* is with you every second, of every minute, of every day.

THOUGHTS

The Abundant Life

`...I am come that they might have life and that they might have *it* more abundantly."

St. John 10:10

All that is in the Universe is God's. Every Christian in the world understands and believes that. This being so, then all Christians should understand and know that he is an abundant God. Since all abundance is God's and since the Paul's advocated "...*and to patience godliness...*" then in order to become like God one must in fact learn to be abundant as God I is abundant. Since we are children of God and all abundance belongs to Him then it stands to reason that all abundance is in fact ours as well.

Why is it that so many Christians live in lack? Notice that I say, so many Christians, not *all* Christians. The only thing that can keep abundance from those that believe in God is their belief or acceptance of some false belief that somehow they are not worthy of abundance or that living in abundance is some kind of sin. God created everything in nature to be abundant and thus all things in nature are abundant. It is only man that allows him or her self to live in lack of what is natural for them to have and obtain.

In order from one to move from a world in which there is lack and neediness into a world of abundance, one must first figure out what is the limiting belief that they have about abundance and release that belief. Once one accepts abundance as God's gift, then the heaven's can open up and pour out abundance to them. This means abundance of money, health, love, relationship and every other needful thing. This transition is instantaneous. God said that is is at the door knocking; if any man will answer He will come in and sup with him.

> *"Ask, and it shall be given you; seek, and ye shall find; knock, and it shall be opened unto you."*
>
> Matt. 7:7

> *"Behold, I stand at the door, and knock: if any man hear my voice, and open the door, I will come in to him, and will sup with him, and he with me."*
>
> Rev. 3:20

To sup with God, is to sit at his table of abundance. Who are the people that you associate with right now? Are they needy or abundant? If you are going to associate with God, you will be doing it at His level. Of course God loves those that are poor and needy; he also loves those that are rich and abundant. If God loves the rich and abundant just as much as those that are poor and needy then one carrying a belief that being rich and abundant is sinful is a false belief and should be cast out. Living with this kind of mindset only serves to keep one poor and needy and does not benefit anyone. It merely limits you from having access to the gifts and blessing of what God has given for your use in this world.

Is it government's responsibility to save people from poverty? Why is so many are impoverished while many others are abundant? People that are living in poverty don't need more welfare, they need more inspiration. When they are inspired and have hope that they too can partake of the abundance that God has given all of us, they will in fact be able to be abundant as well. It first starts with understanding that they have that opportunity, that they can release limiting and false beliefs about their right and their ability to have abundance and instilling in them the hope and belief that they can achieve such. Government welfare programs do noting to inspire anyone to success. In fact, the opposite is true. Once on the government dole, moving up the financial ladder hurts those using the system. To truly become financial stable, one has to break away from government welfare and take the yoke upon their own shoulders to accomplish financial freedom.

To become like God is to become independent of others for support in ones well-being as well as ones material wants, needs and desires. There are those who because of mental, emotional or other substantial reason will need assistance and support from those who are living in abundance. This is part of the gift of God, that of sharing with those who are in need. Of course, this sharing process also causes another affect which is; the person who does the giving will have more abundance added to them. It is God's way! Whatever one gives, it is returned to them ten-fold. Those that envy the rich and abundant are ignoring the fact that God always blesses the giver. You can never out give God. Every time one gives, God gives back to them multiplied and thus those that envy the rich will only envy them more. It is a sadistic cycle that people are in when the envy the rich. If you want to be God-like, give up the disempowering belief that the rich are damned and that only the poor will go to heaven.

When you give up the disempowering beliefs that keep you in poverty, the doors of heaven will open up and abundance can be part of your life. It is a birthright. All God's children, you are one too, are born with the right to partake of the abundance of this world. As people begin to understand this and accept it as being true, poverty will be swept from the face of this Earth. All God's children will live an abundant life when they accept that His abundance as their abundance. Nothing that any of us owns belongs to any of us. It is all God's. We are merely the custodians and keepers in kind of what he has entrusted us with. When God can trust you to use His abundance wisely, it will be poured out upon you and your cup will runneth over.

THOUGHTS

Of Good Report

"Finally, brethren, whatsoever things are true, whatsoever things *are* honest, whatsoever things *are* just, whatsoever things *are* pure, whatsoever things *are* lovely, whatsoever things *are* of good report; if *there be* any virtue, and if *there be* any praise, think on these things."

Philip. 4:8

Followers of Christ have been admonished to think on things that are true, honest, just, pure, lovely, of good report and virtuous. I can think of no other principle being shared with mankind that fits so perfectly all of these attributes more then what is being shared by those practicing the *Law of Attraction*. The whole premise of this *Law* is that whatever your predominant thoughts are is what you are drawing into your life. "Sew a thought, reap an act, sew an act, and reap a habit…"

There are so many things in the world now of a perverse nature being promoted by those who would lead people away from their hopes and dreams. It is timely that there are authors, ministers, philosophers, healers, creative people from all aspects of life and others sharing their experience and knowledge about the *Law of Attraction* and coming forth to help others gain an understanding of this important *Law*.

Of course there are those who will fight against those who are working to shine the light of the *Law of Attraction* on the world. The sooner people become aware that perverse things lead them away from their hopes and dreams and the things that destroy the very soul of man, the more people will abandon those foolish things and begin to empower themselves by taking more care in what they allow their thoughts to be focused on. When you are in darkness you can't at the same time be in the light and when you are in the light, you can not be in the darkness. You can spend time either in the light or in darkness but you can not occupy both places at once. The more time you give to one, the less time you are in the other. So the more time one spends in the light, the more they attract things that are of the light.

> *"No man can serve two masters: for either he will hate the one, and love the other; or else he will hold to the one, and despise the other. Ye cannot serve God and mammon."*

Matt. 6:24

You can always tell who those are the serve mammon. They despise those that believe in righteousness and every now and then, maybe more often then not, their hatred for those that believe really shines. Without really realizing it, their true colors are revealed.

No one who is a faithful believer of Christ is perfect. There are those who believe they are perfect. I have met a few of those people and you probably have too. So for those of us who know we are not perfect and understand that we are still capable of sin yet understand that there is a means to overcome such, the *Law of Attraction* is a principle and *Law* with a promise. "Sew a thought, reap an act..." It is absolutely guaranteed that when you use this law, the outcome will be in perfect alignment with the original action. The original action of course being the thought and the corresponding reaction is the result.

This is why sin is not a spontaneous action. It is the result of previous thoughts that have come to fruition and the outcome is always the same. You have been distracted and have been swayed from the path that leads to your hopes and dreams. One must become aware of the fact that they must change the focus of their thoughts to those things they truly want in life which is their hopes and dreams and slowly but surely they will overcome those thoughts that lead to the destruction of those hopes and dreams.

What do people hope for?

Everyone has different hopes and dreams. We all have hopes and dreams of what we want to do and have in this life. We also have things that we hope for in the life to come. This life is only one step in our journey along the path of eternal life. It is not the end... it is not the beginning... it is an intricate part of a grand journey.

One thing that I have discovered is this; you can not achieve anything that you do NOT believe in. Just because you do not believe in something, does not mean it does not exist or is not real. We all have things in our life that were not real years ago but they exist now. At one time the world was flat. There are still people who go through life living life in such a way that for them, everything is flat. For them there is no possibility of anything except the things they can see, hear, taste, smell or touch. They go around believing the world is flat and will not believe otherwise until they see it first hand.

For those that believe, without seeing, they are more blessed. These people get to experience things in life that others find un-believable. It doesn't matter that one is experiencing more wealth, health and happiness to these people. There has to be some reason that people who have it all, have it all. They have to be doing something wrong. They have to be cheating people. They have to be up to no good. There is no way they can have these things just because they believe they can.

When those that do not have everything they want in life understand that it IS a matter of believing and that the *Law of Attraction* is one of the most important laws within their grasp to know and understand and they seek to understand and use it, they will begin to have the windows of heaven opened up to them. Their cup will overflow. They will have more then enough for their own needs and they will be able to share that abundance with others.

"For we are saved by hope: but hope that is seen is not hope: for what a man seeth, why doth he yet hope for? But if we hope for that we see not, then do we with patience wait for it."

Rom. 8:24-25

Increase the things you hope for. Increase your knowledge of the *Law of Attraction* and how you can use this law to achieve greater health, wealth and happiness and with patience wait for it. Focus your attention on those things that will continue to nurture and replenish that hope and in time the manifestation of that hope will be realized. Stay away from things that are devised to distract you from that final hope. Whether it be the hope of things you want in this life or the hope of things you wish for in the life to come, do not allow yourself to be distracted.

Can you build upon these hopes and dreams?

Absolutely! As you learn to use the Law of Attraction to create more health, wealth and happiness in this life, you will gain power to attract even more. Can you become perfect? That may or may not be achievable in this life, however it is the final outcome of what we all hope for in the life to come. Eternal life is a life that allows us to do all things, see all things, hope for all things and be all things.

Life in heaven is supposed to offer endless possibilities. That is... things that have no end and that are eternal. What is your hope for eternal life?

Is it one that has endless possibilities? Is it a hope that allows you to have things that are infinite in nature? Are family and friends forever? Is it possible? Anything is possible to they that believeth.

> "Jesus said unto him, if thou canst believe, all things *are* possible to him that believeth."

> Mark 9:23

The only one that can limit the things that you have in this life or the life to come is you. With God all things are possible. That being so the only person that can limit that possibility is you and you alone. What one person may expect and receive in this life is dependent on their own belief in what they can have in this life. The same is true in the life to come. Limit what you believe you can have in the life to come, and you limit yourself to what you can receive there. Just because you do not see a thing, does not mean it does not exist. *"To him that believeth, all things are possible."*

THOUGHTS

Carmen J. Day

The Vibration of Expectancy is Patience

...and "let us not be weary in well doing: for in due season we shall reap, if we FAINT not."

Galatians 6:9

In my daily mediations, prayer and conversations with God, I am often reminded to have faith. Stay the course; be unwavering in my desires and dedication in my walk."

When I was asked to co-author this book, *Mastery of Abundant Living* for Christians, my enthusiasm was all that was necessary to say, YES, actually honored to do such work. What a wonderful way to serve by offering my love, sharing the wisdom, and giving the inspired word as revealed. "Certainly, I am willing and yes, it is good."

What happens as you begin to think of the task, and the mind begins to inform and taunt you? "Who do you think you are? You can not right...You do not know enough, you are not ready... You are having problems yourself... how are you going to help someone else?" These are the mind fields that will cause yourself to doubt, or even question your authority. This, my friend is when the REAL work begins. As you move forward in manifesting your desires, realizing your dreams the deceptive manipulation that the mind plays, can cause you to fatigue and faint. Conquering the battlefield of the mind is to renew your *self* by breathing life into the situation. In controlling that part of you, where error thinking originates, Satan lies, sin or whatever name you call the dim side of your mind, is to overcome your debilitating thoughts and not grow weak and faint.

To faint is just give up! It is talking yourself out of a divine blessing and opportunity to be the authentic you. It takes more than to be enthusiastic about what you want to create; it takes an innate understanding of the process for which creation thrives. We must allow the room for our dreams to manifest.

Here is what I mean…when the mistake in our thoughts first rears its ugly head…squelch it immediately. Speak life, speak truth into the situation. Affirm through meditations and prayer who and who you are. The "well-doing" is a continually proclamation that you are the light in the world to light up the world. There is and will NEVER be another you! Within you is greater than that which is in the world, which seeks to destroy my gifts and talents…Speak truth, speak life into your thoughts. It is breathing light into the darkest place we will ever encounter…our mind!

I spoke life into my mistaken thoughts with

something like this... In a quiet place, I had taken a deep satisfying breath and within the peace, I began with...

"*God, Master of all there is - creator of all things tangible and intangible... how great thou art, how magnificent thy Holy name is. You love me so much and being an excellent, wonderful and loving father, you sent your Son, "the way shower" to be my example. Knowing that the Holy Spirit have its being in me, as me to be a blessing, to be prosperous, to embody the treasures of abundant living...I am who you say that I AM. I AM an excellent writer, right now... within my mind is the inspired word that burns my heart with passion and intensity! It spills over from a never ending reservoir though every cell within my body...exploding with thunder to reveal great mysteries of our love affair. I feel the vibration within my hands, and know that each word is inspired creating the vibration of penmanship excellence! I AM an author of word art that is inspired by the breath of we... I AM the light for the power within me lights up every dark place, there NO weapon formed against me shall prosper, I take control of my thoughts, as I have dominion over all things upon this earth! I know and love who I AM. I give thanks, and I am so very grateful that as I have created this thing, I am attracting all opportunities to express my love for you. YES!!! I believe who you say I AM. My gratitude fills my entire being and the word goes forth...Amen!*"

The vibration of that love song, sung in my heart has created the vibration of expectancy! I expected the spirit of God to flow through me, as me for sharing the love of God...I expected that as I placed pen to paper...well nails to computer; my melody would fill the pages with such a beautiful song. While expressing from an authentic place within my soul the majestic wonder of my walk with of God. My appreciation for his love, and the Laws placed within our universe in order for me to fully enjoy my earthly pleasures. I am a divine scripter, here being a servant of the Most High that is all I need to know.

As a *Master of Abundant Living* seeker, remember expectancy is the expectation for the Law of Attraction to manifest anything in your experience.

What are you giving your energy to? Better yet do you know what you are consciously or subconsciously expecting, right now?

When you speak the word, it goes out into the Universe and does not come back void. Meaning... it is all ready done in the mind of God, all that is required of you ask and receive. This is done with faith and expectancy.

I have heard many people say, "you know I am doing all the right things that this book says, or that DVD movie purports, but nothings happens for me, it is not working for me. It is hocus-pocus, boloney."

You will manifest much faster when you can keep most of the weed (err thoughts) out of the garden (your mind)...Meaning, your thoughts can maintain a perfect garden, and your thoughts can destroy it. Mastery of Abundant Living for Christians, Carmen J. Day says...*Patience is the missing key!*

> *"For ye have need of patience, that, after ye have done the will of God, ye might receive the promise."*
>
> Hebrews 10:36

> *"But if we hope for that we see not, then do we with patience wait for it."*
>
> Romans 8:25

Patience, being an important virtues to abundant living and requests our intentional mastery because, as you send out the desires of your heart through prayer, meditation, contemplation, conversation or/ and thoughts the universe automatically responds with the sacred, "YES" without fail. We know that the desires of your heart are perfect and acceptable will of God, and all things ask is granted when we ask, right? Then what happens when your requests seem to be not heard or answered...or they do not manifest when we think they should?

This is an important piece to remember; all...ALL

requests are answered. I believe that all physical manifestation enters into your experience when you maintain/dwell in the vibration of expectancy. What vibration signal are you sending out?

For instance, if you were to plant some corn...with the desire to harvest an excellent crop of corn, instead of reading or understanding the incubation stages for it to mature, you get angry, upset and frustrated...and uproots the seeds from the soil, before the appointed time. We can learn all of God's Laws of the Universe by paying attention to nature's way. What will you have after ripping the seeds out of its appointed incubation? Yes...no corn.

Many of us do that with life challenges. We get tired, and faint before the harvest...Oftentimes the biggest part of the wait is over, and just before the finish line, we pass out. In just one more step, the invisible finish line would have appeared and you walk away as the victor. What would that say about what we are focusing our attention on? Failing? Unworthiness? Fear? Doubt? Worry? How about the classic....What others would think about me?

In the mind of God, there is no time as we understand it. The stronger the vibration on the desired expectancy...the faster in which the Law of Attraction will work to physically bring it to you. Your signal, your vibration, your frequency is always on...and creating, tarring down, rebuilding, uprooting, replanting...on and on. What a ride we take the universe on. We create our delays because we faint in heart.

> *"So that we ourselves glory in you in the churches of God for your patience and faith in all your persecutions and tribulations that ye endure:*
>
> *Which is a manifest token of the righteous judgment of God, that ye may be counted worthy of the Kingdom of God, for which ye also suffer."*

2 Thessalonians 1:4-5

THOUGHTS

_____

_____

_____

_____

_____

_____

_____

_____

_____

_____

_____

Inspirational
Stories

Beauty and Possibilities

by Rhonda

I am a daughter of the King (Father God), and as His daughter, he wants only the best for me. The Law of Attraction has helped me to want--and know how to achieve--the best for Myself!

Even as a Christian for most of my 50 years, I never really saw the beauty and possibilities of the world until I adopted the LOA and incorporated it into my spiritual beliefs as well.

For years, I felt that being a Christian meant I had to suffer . . . but didn't God say "Suffer not little children?"

It occurred to me that, as earthly, mortal reflections of Him, He wants us to be happy, productive, optimistic, effervescent, successful and joyful! He doesn't want us to spend our days moping, worrying, being sad, thinking negative thoughts . . . what kind of Christian testimony is THAT? Who'd want to be a Christian if THAT's all they saw in us?

Since becoming a practitioner of the LOA, people stop me and comment on my positive attitude every day. I'm far more grateful--REALLY grateful--for all the things I've received from Father God, and by acknowledging him as the Source Energy for all these things.

My career is flourishing. My relationship with my children and my friends is better than I could have ever imagined. To me, the Law of Attraction was the missing link in my being able to truly live the life a believer should live and to set the kind of examples that God wants us to be to other people who may not yet know him!

On more than one occasion, I've heard other followers of the LOA say that people around them say, "Whatever it is you're drinking that makes you so positive (so calm, so happy, etc.), I want some of it!"

BINGO! That's how God wants His children to be viewed!

"You can change your beliefs so they

empower your dreams and desires.

Create a strong belief in yourself

and what you want."

Marcia Wieder

It is important that you feel good

by Laura

I am a follower of Jesus the Christ, and consider Him, in the form of the Holy Spirit to be my Ultimate Master, Mentor, Teacher, Guide and Lord. He has had me on this journey for 30 years that I've been aware of........probably longer! :) Jesus was the one, whom the God of the Universe chose to introduce me to Himself. I am not ashamed to be his follower, although I am not part of an organized church system, as we know it in the western civilization. Through His help, I believe I have been in a process of awakening to the reality that is not of this temporal world we see all around us.

I will attempt to share some thoughts regarding being a Christian who practices the Law of Attraction:

I believe over years of the journey he has continually had me on a course of "Mind Renewal" - basically taking on HIS MIND. The Kingdom of God IS within us, and I believe if we are a part of His Body, then we also have His mind. He's been teaching me that it's a continual practice of "Mind washing" by HIS word, and not only just the Bible and/or New Testament. He has been my "Chief Shepherd" and has been faithful to feed me safely on the High Mountains of the Spirit, by a one on one relationship with Him. He has fed me and led me to some VERY wonderful teachings that have literally transformed my life. They've ALL been HIS WORD, as they have had the ability to transform my mind, having more Joy, more Peace, and most of all more Love and forgiveness! Through his help having the ability to let him uproot the old mind patterns through things we've been taught in our lives by "Carnal Mind sets".

This has put a SPRING in my STEP, a SMILE on my FACE, and a SONG in my HEART. I'm a singer/songwriter/musician, as well as a piano teacher of 40 students. I have NEVER had to advertise to get more students - it's all word of mouth. I love the kids, and I know they've been attracted to keep coming back week after week for more reasons than just learning music. They leave lessons with a smile on their face, a spring in their step, and a song in their hearts too. Just sharing some practical areas in which knowing God and practicing the LOA, has been a fruitful experience. I might add that because of my experience with God over the years, the LOA really has been a natural law for me, before I even knew what to call it. :) It's just SO great to see these truths coming to light on such a GRAND SCALE in these days!

"Setting our affections on the things that are from ABOVE and not of this world, cause ALL good things to come to us!" It has been quoted that Jesus said not to WORRY about what you are going to wear or what you will eat but, "Seek First the Kingdom of God and His righteousness and all these things would be added to us." What is the Kingdom, but Righteousness, Peace and JOY in the Holy Ghost! All these things are wonderful, and to quote one of the teachers of "The Secret" - "It's important that you FEEL GOOD." This all goes SO hand in hand with the teachings of Christ.

While Jesus served His time here on the earth, He seemed to be SO big on providing for people and taking care of their needs. I LOVE that about HIm. There's nothing wrong with having all that we need - the key is not to become attached to those things, and place them as FIRST place in our lives. If we can FIRST find our true peace and happiness in the things we don't see, then ALL the material things will automatically flow in our direction.

To quote another wonderful teacher, "Except for God's Love, we need nothing, and he who needs nothing can be trusted with everything."

There is SO much, and this is such a very deep and rich subject, worthy to explore! The Law of Attraction is a truth that absolutely cannot be denied, no matter what religion you may follow. I believe Jesus himself would have agreed with the teaching. The fact is, back in Jesus day, much of science was not yet discovered - there was no electricity, so explaining to the people back then about "Energy" or "Magnetic Attraction" would have been inconceivable! God has brought this race to the place NOW where we can truly understand some of the deeper things (not all) that Jesus said concerning things he could not share, for there was no way for the people to conceive them.

I'm truly excited about this NEW DAY that we are

blessed to be a part of!

ALL roads lead to one Truth - GOD IS!

"You do not have to be superhuman

to do what you believe in."

Debbie Fields

Be Careful What You Wish For

Deborah M. Buchanan

Throughout my life I was always inspired by other people. Being inspired doesn't always mean in a good way. Many people have showed me what I don't want to be as well but for the most part I've been around people who have something in their life or about them that inspires me. I used to think I knew it all and found out there was so much more I needed to know for my growth and I don't feel that will ever end. I've always said "don't envy people; instead learn how they came to be who they are". Envy is a waste of time, you could miss out on something that could better your life by being envious, instead be *Inspired*, that's the way I choose to live my life. If there's anything I've learned along the way I feel a passion to share that with other people so maybe they too can take a piece of that and better their life in a certain area. I live to be *inspired*.

The stories that have been collected for this book have *inspired* me in one way or another. From every story I took something away with me. It's my wish for you that you as well will learn something from all of these stories. We all have our good times and times we would rather live without, that's just a part of life and growing. These are real people with real stories, what a better way to learn and to grow than from the experience of another.

Nothing in my life has ever happened by *coincidence*, I truly believe that. Every situation I found myself in was meant to be, every person I've met and known in my life were there for a reason, I believe that with all my heart. With every situation, with every person you take another step in life.

I was born to a very wealthy mother but the silver spoon was removed very quickly, so quickly that I don't even remember it being there. Nothing ever really came that easily and when it did come at times I didn't appreciate it, I took it for granted. I've now learned that you take nothing for granted and *gratitude* is so important. Without *gratitude* you lose your chance of having more come into your life to appreciate and be grateful for. What always amazed me was that I always had the right person in my life at the right time. I was always in the right place at the right time. I'll forever be grateful for that. My Angels have definitely watched over me and led me in my steps so who am I to regret any of it?

Along my path I've also learned that there's ways to make things happen. I'm not the most patient person in the world, never have been, that's a part of me that needs work. I've used several techniques through my life to get what I wanted. One technique was *creative visualization*. I was doing it without even knowing I was doing it. I'd see things as if they have already happened. I've always loved to dream and have a vivid imagination. That blended with visualizing and worked for me, I made many things happen, still do. Visualization is a very powerful and some what unused gift we all have. You do however have to believe in what you see in your mind. There were times I didn't even have to have such belief because the visions would just come to my mind and I just knew that the vision would manifest because it came too easily to me I didn't have to push it.

Another technique I've had so much success with was *writing* my dreams. I'd write them again as if they had already happened. Writing is great for the imagination. Once you begin writing, the thoughts come at top speed and you keep writing with ease. It is all about knowing what you want then writing about it and may I add in detail. Details are very important. I once wrote about an apartment I wanted in complete detail down to how it would be decorated, the price and area. I didn't leave anything out. I handed the paper to my very close friend Stephanie to read and unknown to me she kept it. Seven months later I had told her I found an apartment that I loved and she then handed me the paper. I was shocked that she kept it all that time but that's Stephanie. I was amazed as she was because I had gotten everything I wrote about down to the smallest detail. What didn't amaze me was seeing Stephanie and my other dear friend Joanie with pen and paper in hand writing away. I've always preached writing your dreams and goals. I recently taught this technique to my ex husband Frank who knowing him had to wonder to himself "why didn't you tell me this years go". I didn't know years ago. I came across a great book on it which I will list in suggested reading and learned the technique that way and since have inspired others to do the same. I cannot stress how powerful the written word is. A few words of caution - be careful what you wish for, for that's how powerful this technique is. Write it down and put it away. I wish I could tell you a time limit but I can't, it just works.

I've always prayed and maybe it was those prayers that got me through life. Of course I pray to the Divine / God and my angels and spirit guides, yes we all have our own angels and spirit guides so don't ever ignore your inner voice because that is when they make themselves known. I've also prayed to The Saints, my favorite and he never fails me is St. Anthony. If you ever lose anything just talk to St. Anthony and watch how quickly you find what you're looking for, he's an amazing spirit. St. Anthony is the patron Saint of lost articles and since the word 'lost' is in there I also pray to him when I feel lost, he comes through every time. Another favorite Saint of mine is St. Jude the patron Saint for the hopeless. We all feel hopeless at times. There's a particular Saint for every want and need. You do have to pray to them with conviction you can't just say "hey I need your help", no it doesn't work that way although I've been praying to St. Anthony for so long I tend to just talk to him. I also tend to just talk to God.

Everyone has their way of manifesting what they want, some like I had said don't even know their doing it, good or bad and that's where The Law of Attraction comes in, a subject I am deeply into right now and trying to perfect.

The Law of Attraction states that whatever thought were sending out we get the same back. If the thought and feeling is positive you get positive, if the thought and feeling are negative well you get negative in return. It's a subject that's also very powerful and I suggest everyone learn its technique.

Throughout this book you'll read about several different techniques and how they've worked for people. It's my hope that by reading these stories you'll read a technique that sparks something in you, that resonates with your spirit. Remember, nothing is impossible. I will repeat myself because this is so important, be careful what you wish, pray for, and write for - because you just may get it.

"There are two ways to live your life
One is as though nothing is a miracle
The other is as though everything
is a miracle."

Einstein

Be Open and Ready

Susanna Z, Nova Scotia, Canada

Despite some bad choices, my life was good and I wouldn't trade any of it. For as long as I can remember I have asked God, the Universe, someone, anyone at all to bring in to my life the one person who is my soul-mate, my mentor.

To no avail, as much as I kept looking, listening, hoping, just figured God had better things to do. In the year of 2005, God pulled me out of a bad situation in the nick of time. For a split second I had opened the window to let the sunshine through the window in to the darkness I was living. It was only that one split second He needed to grab me by the hand and take the lead. I could do no other then follow.

I started rebuilding my life and thought I was doing good, when I was brought to my knees. I had to quite my job of only three months, and all of this a little less then a month before Christmas. To make matters worse, so I thought, my then male friend broke up with me. I cried three days straight couldn't stop, no matter how I tried.

At this point I figured God had forgotten about me,

but it was not going to change how I felt about Him. Still every night I would pray in desperation for anything, anyone, the one person that would be able to pull me up and out of where I was. The bottomless barrel and I was about to fall deeper. I just got through telling the father of my children that he will have to make sure the children knew I was going to be alright.

In 2005, on December 23rd before retiring to bed, I checked email one more time, not really sure why. There it was, an email which has changed my life forever, it was a business proposition. I have not looked back ever since.

It fell through but that is fine because I now know it was the tool which God had used to answer my life long prayers, for my soul-mate and mentor.

In my despair the soul was open and ready to finally receive that which was meant for me all along. Yes, God knew all along there was a plan for us to work together. As to what, how, where and when I will not question, it too will be revealed in due time.

The Law of Attraction works, but you have to be open and ready to receive. Who ever you are, never falter from the path you know is right.

You may get what you seek tomorrow, in a week or

almost 40 years later, not before God and the Universe know of dealing with what is to come. Keep giving no matter what, and learn to receive.

Above all be grateful, believe and trust that you too will receive. It is the Law of the Attraction.

"Imagination is the beginning of creation.
You imagine what you desire,
you will what you imagine and at last
you create what you will."

George Bernard Shaw

Magic Pouch

Joan G, Glencove, NY

My husband passed away suddenly on our wedding anniversary from a heart attack and for the nine years after, I haven't had a date. I of course did want to date men but nothing was happening and I couldn't figure out why, I just assumed maybe it wasn't my time. Nine years later I realized it was my time had been all along.

I made myself a little pouch filled with rose petals and rose quartz crystals and called it my magic pouch. Every time I held the pouch or looked at it I had feelings of being in love again. I carried this pouch in my purse wherever I went and when I felt doubtful I'd hold my pouch and tell myself it was coming. I started to take long hot baths because that's the way I relax and put some headphones and listen to love songs as I envisioned in my mind a man. I never put a face on him but it was always the same vision of me and him together. I did this over and over again. I also started playing love songs in my car wherever I went and held onto that vision.

All of a sudden, within months I was dating. I had an urge to take out a personal ad which I never dreamed I'd do and started getting responses. I went on a few dates with a few different men but nothing worked out. I still held my vision and still carried and held my pouch that I truly believed would bring me the man I wanted; it was a tool for me.

I met a very nice man but there were no sparks so we ended the date as friends. Months later he called and wanted to see me again and something made me go. I had a great time but yet didn't feel he was the man of my dreams. We continued dating and all I knew was that I was having fun when out of the blue I began having feelings for this man. This happened only months after making my good luck charm so to speak and began seeing myself in a relationship. I realized I was in love with him and he told me the same and we dated for 2 years. Were now happily married and now believe that to see something in my mind over and over again will bring to me what I want because after nine years of not having a date it didn't look hopeful, but then again I wasn't hopeful or focusing on it.

"In the province of the mind, what one
believes to be true either is true
or becomes true."

John Lilly

Vision of Winning

Chris B, Bohemia, NY

I'm 18 years old and have always played football. I was a great football player in high school and even as a kid but my coaches were just so bad and we didn't win many games when I was younger. When I was 10 years old I was on a team that never won a game and we were in the middle of the season. This really bothered me.

I talked to my mom about it and she told me to go into my room light a white candle and turn out the lights and lay back and picture my team winning the next day. Of course I thought this was weird but I wanted it so bad I did it. I pictured my team winning by a long shot and of course me being the star player of that game. I really did see all of this in my head and I was getting excited like it was really happening.

The next day we played the game. Our team won by a long shot and also for the first time ever since I started football and had never did this again I ran a 52 yard touchdown. The crowd was screaming, my team mates lifted me up in the air and it felt great. It was just as I saw it. That was an experience I'll never forget.

"The thing always happens that you really believe in; and the belief in a thing makes it happen."

Frank Lloyd Wright

Faith in the Divine

Michele J, Attica NY

I lie here in the tranquil evening silence as the rain taps on my window. The beating of my heart is the tempo in the night. I watch the rain and think about how wonderful life really is. Relating life to nature, I say a silent prayer. I'm thankful for the storms, for in return   there   is   growth.

All the pain I've endured in the past, made me grow. My eyes have been opened to a world full of sunshine where life was once so dark. I think of all the days I cried, asking "Why?" Unanswered questions raced through my mind because I did not understand the things that broke my heart. I grew weak as I was led astray to a world where clouds hung over and tore me in two. Throughout it all, I came closer to my death. With no destination I wanted   to   die.

Then on one lonely night He came to me and took me to the ocean. As I gazed upon the water, I saw a reflection, an image of insanity, an image of sadness. A flooding of sorrow filled my heart and I longed to make   the   image   a   happy   one.

He led me closer and I realized it wasn't just an

image in my mind. It was a reflection in the waters. Nature's mirror! The reflection of me! A teardrop fell like the rain of tonight and soon I created a flood. A storm so intense, I cried to myself upon the sandy shore. I looked up to the darkened sky and saw only one bright star. Throughout the darkness of the night, there was still a flicker of light created by that star. It was then that I knew my creator was with me, that I wasn't alone. A glimpse of hope dried my eyes as I realized, throughout the pain, there's faith to believe. A faith so strong, all my weakness disappeared as time went by.

As the morning light approached me, darkness faded. Strength took over the sorrow, and the image was gone. Only a reflection of beauty was to be seen as the water resembled hammered gold beneath the sun.

The storm brought beauty. The pain brought strength. And life brought love. For without faith, there is never a destination. And without Him, there is no life.

"I am a woman in process. I'm just trying like everybody else. I try to take every conflict, every experience, and learn from it. Life is never dull."

Oprah Winfrey

Writing to My Angels

Tracy I, Patchogue, NY

Years ago I was in a relationship from which I had my son. The relationship didn't work out and I was left a single mom with a new baby, a run down car and a low paying job. I moved back home because I really had no choice in order to make ends meet.

While living home I became involved a few years later in another relationship which lasted for seven years. I was madly in love with him and of course wanted to settle down with this man. He was afraid of commitment and never really entertained the thought of us settling down. He was an excellent role model for my son and the relationship was good in all other aspects so I figured in time he would commit. I was wrong. Seven years into this relationship I found out he was seeing another woman. I was heart broken to say the least. I felt more pain than I've ever felt in my life.

I lived in New York at the time and decided I just couldn't live there anymore; it was as if I was running away. My family and I moved to Florida in hopes of a better life and to forget my pain and also my son's pain as they were very close. Little did I know that there was a higher power leading me to make that move and for a bigger reason. I was 35 at the time and had never been married and this was very depressing to me.

For my first year in Florida I went into a deep depression. Everything was so different and I missed home in NY. I was working at a job I didn't like, traveling in an old car what seemed like forever to get to that job and still not meeting anyone. I had no friends to share my pain or express it to, only my family. I was becoming more distraught by the day thinking these were the cards God dealt me and I finally just gave up.

I sat one night literally in tears feeling my dreams would never come true. I was now 36, never married and now also miserable where I lived and wanted to go back home to NY but couldn't.

At that point I lit a candle, took a good glance over at my statue of Venus the goddess of love and just began writing. I wrote for hours listing all the qualities I wanted in a man and praying to my angels to please bring him to me. I then buried the list in my drawer and cried my eyes out for the rest of the night and many times after that. I felt that list was my last resort. I was no longer looking for a man. I felt if my angels and higher powers wanted me to have one in my life then they knew I wrote the list and would bring him to me and I left it at that.

Lonely days, weeks and months went by when I got an urge to take out a personal ad on the internet, something I never thought I would ever do but had this incredible urge to do so. I received a few responses and went on a few dates and it was all the same, player after player. I was ready to give up on this too being that my heart was being broken again. Another email had come in and honestly I didn't even want to look at it, perhaps another player? The next day however I did look at it. I wasn't too impressed but yet something kept telling me to write back so I did. I still wasn't that impressed but felt the need to keep writing him back. We wrote back and forth for about a month but believe me my hopes weren't up, there was just this strange urge.

The day came when we finally met and to my surprise I did really like him but kept my cool because I wouldn't allow myself to be hurt again. After several dates my guard had went down, for some reason I felt a comfort with him that I had never felt before.

We dated for two years and I'm very happy to say today were happily married. He is truly my soul-mate. I had a huge beautiful wedding and cried through the whole thing because I couldn't believe this was happening to me. I recently went back and took out my list and went over it only to find he had every single quality I had written down, every one.

I always believed in my angels even through the very hard times and believed in writing your dreams; I was just too lazy and caught up in my own misery until that night. Today before I do anything I ask my angels. If something is wrong I write to them. I totally trust in the angels and always will; they took my written prayer and brought it to my higher power.

"You create your own universe
as you go along."

Winston Churchill

The Law of Attraction

Ramon, CA

When I first saw "The Secret" movie, I was blown away. It gave me chills down my spine. I got so excited and started thinking to myself, "The things and people I have experienced is because I have attracted them in to my life." I then realized that through the Law attraction certain people and certain things came in to my life, the good and the bad. So if I had bad things happen to me it is because I focused my attention on it with thought, feeling and into action. And therefore I attracted it into my life experience. And it works the same way with good.

So with my story, the way the law of attraction has worked for me in a positive way for example is that, I wanted to start a landscaping business. Once my thought and feelings came into place, I then took action to learn more and talked about it more with others and then these two other people found out about me through word of mouth. These two people called me to talk about starting the business with me. And now these two people are my business partners. I didn't realize that I had attracted these two business partners in my life through the law of attraction until after I discovered "The Secret".

I even use the law of attraction to find the perfect house for me and my family. And within one week of deciding to find a house, I had attracted the right person to provide that perfect house for us. Everyday I visualized that house and feeling the feelings of already having it and then made a few telephone calls. And I know why it was so easy getting our house.

What happens is, is that when you focus on something with so much passion, it makes it happen easier and faster for you. Sometimes we might find ourselves struggling in life or with trying to do something. We struggle because our desires are not fully aligned with the universe.

Another thing that we have to keep in mind and practice daily is that nothing new and great can come into our lives without first being grateful for the things that we already have. When we are grateful for things then that brings in good feelings and that can turn into happiness and that will attract more good feelings and good things. Sometimes if we find ourselves unhappy with something, it is because we are comparing things with how they should have been or how they could have been or how they would have been. So instead of comparing things we must be grateful for even the little things in life.

I live my life from the law of attraction every day. I'm attracting like- minded people and want to share and empower with others. I'm living proof that if you change your thoughts, you will change your feelings and change your actions. Then you will transform your life the way it should be.

"All that we are is the result
of what we have thought."

Buddha

God Will Find You a Way with Faith

Jon, New Mexico

I was set to do a book signing in Lubbock, Texas on a Friday night. I was driving from Albuquerque and stopped for gas in Tucumcari, New Mexico. I tried to use my credit card and it didn't work. I had just enough cash to get me to Lubbock. I did not have enough to spend the night, much less get home.

As the store paid me in cash, I would have to sell 20 books just to have enough to have a place to stay. I thought about it for a minute, prayed on it and then kept heading east. Needless to say, I sold 33.

Writing is about faith sometimes. Much of my writing is about heartbreak and despair, and yet I am able to sell my books through a positive attitude. So when you are in your own private Tucumcari, keep on going, God will find a way to get you where you're going!

"What power this is I cannot say.
All that I know is that it exists."

Alexander Graham Bell

Conquering Subconscious Thoughts

Kat C, Gilbert, Arizona

I was thinking.... there are some who have more problems with manifestations than others. Could it be that some of us who perhaps haven't conquered our subconscious thoughts are manifesting on that level? On the level where all the noise is.... the negative thoughts, etc. The place where all of our old patters sit? Perhaps one of the steps to good manifestation is meditation.

In meditation we can take ourselves to the most wonderful places and conquer those negative thoughts for awhile and with the habit of meditation everyday perhaps the positive we feel when we visit in our minds those wonderful places will start to be a part of our subconscious mind. When negative thoughts do enter our heads at some point we can then have a tool to conquer them.

"I feel uncomfortable when I
am experiencing change,
if I don't feel uncomfortable
I am not changing.
To become a better person
I must experience change."

Bruce Goldwell

He Gave His Life to God

Bob

I was an ADD child and now I am an ADHD man. School was very hard for me because I was set back in the first grade and always had that low esteem profile because of all the sneers from the other kids. My parents where average and wanted the best for me, but they were average and no-one knew about ADD. My dad was a womanizer type of guy and always had to go somewhere and left me home when I would ask to go with him. I blamed myself because I had bad teeth, was chubby, and had a lisp when I spoke. My mom and he fought a lot and it was always scary at my house. I was the oldest of 4 kids and was made to watch over the rest when the parents were out and about. I always felt alone but in charge and not in charge, if you understand the thoughts of a little boy.

I was a bully as a young boy and my friends dad tolerated me because almost all of their dads worked for my dad at the air base (us air force base) He was a top sergeant in the air force and they were under him because of their rank.

I couldn't pay attention in class and had love sickness bad. I would always fall for some girl and would think about her all day and even dream about her. I had to take a lot of drugs as a kid because I always was sick, I didn't know I was allergic to milk, too. My teeth got bad, plus, brushing them was not a priority at our house. My dad was a tyrant when he was home. He was as mean as they come and was ashamed of me for who and what I was. He made me sit with my back to the television while we ate our supper and the rest of the family got to watch it. We were poor and food was a problem. I was always hungry and was addicted to everything that tasted good and that was sweet.

He would punish us by taking the television away from us for having bad grades and it taught me to be a thief. I would sit and ponder about things I could do and would sneak out at night and do them. I learned how to break into places and get away before getting caught. I only had one girl friend that ever really cared for me and she was my older cousin. She was 21 and I was 16. My dad wanted her and it became a competition for us to see who was going to have her and he hated me that I was the one she chose. As sick as it seems, that's me at 16 in my dysfunctional family.

I left school when I turned 18 because I was going to fail again and I just couldn't stand myself. I had a taste of life outside of school and was already drinking, doing drugs, having sex, and I had my own car. I left school and went to work for my dad as a garage mechanic and so on. It was better than school, but I knew I was going no-where fast. I had mostly older girl friends that would take me out and show me off. I looked good back then.

I went into the air force, became a jet engine welder, and went to Vietnam. I came back home on leave and married the girl I use to flirt with that worked across the street from me. She was a cook at the service window in a small restaurant. We had become on and off letter writers while I was in Vietnam. I married her in the 2 weeks after I came home. She was a trophy wife that my dad fell in love with. He took his time but eventually made his move on her and she gave in to keep the peace in the family (that's what she said). All I know is that it was a long time ordeal that I had had my suspicions about and finally realized that something really is going on with those two.

I am going to leave out about 15 years and get to the part about me. I tried to get her to get to counseling so we could work on ourselves, but it was like pulling teeth, so I gave up. I had started venturing out and meeting other ladies…it's sad, but I was lonely and hurt by all that I lived with. I had 30 affairs by the time. I became a drunk with anger that I couldn't control anymore. I never hit my wife but I put holes in the walls and broke doors and scared my kids so bad that they were afraid of me. They never told me that, but I know deep down inside I hurt them with words and my cursing.

I divorced my first wife. I paid all my child support that I was suppose to pay and I even paid for my kids to receive counseling so they could understand that they were not the problem and that it was every body around them. I was told to go to AA by my therapist or I was going to be put in jail.

I went to AA and that's where I met Sue, my present wife. We had to work really hard to get where we are in our marriage. We did counseling separate from one another and with couples and in groups. We finally got out of all that and I am finally free of my obligation to the courts. We attend AA conventions and do retreats together and sometimes Sue goes with her lady friends without the guys. It's all good stuff. I even pay to send those that don't have the money so they might come to understand what these retreats are all about. I guess Sue and I have sent at least seven persons on these retreats. To make a long story short, we live the AA life and it's easier for us today because we know how to get help.

I have done a lot of damage to a lot of people and I have tried to make amends to them all. I know this is impossible but God knows what's in my heart today. This is only a fraction of my life's story and I hope it explains me. I did go back and get my high school diploma and even got some college under my belt. I have learned about ADHA and have accepted that I am what I am and that's what I work on and I don't beat myself up over it. I also understand that I have become the teacher for those that need direction away from addiction. Sue and I live this life to help others. Sue is also a RN at the local hospital. She is really a healer of the body and the helper for those wanting to learn how to get a peace of mind.

I took up flying back in 1985 and then stopped because it got so expensive. I started back again in 2002 and decided this not for me and looked into gyrocopters, which was my real dream. I have been gyro'ing for five years now and love it. Like I said, this is only a small part of my history.

I did the church thing and searched for the church that made sense to me. It was a long rough road checking out all the denominations and trying to understand their creeds. There were plenty of nights of tears for me trying to get a grip on life and its terms.

At one point I turned away from God and cursed him. At another point I asked him to give me my dad's pain and he did. I also asked God to give it back to him because I was just making it with my own set of troubles.

I owe it all to God and JESUS CHRIST. It was my faith in him and believing in him that got me through my whole ordeal. God carried me and he also gave me my wife and my church and my life and an adult way of thinking. May God bless you!

"Take chances.
When rowing forward,
the boat may rock."

Chinese Proverb

Affirming Love

Katherine F, Ronkonkoma, NY

I was sitting at my desk at work one day during some down time and decided to write in my affirmation book. While writing I started thinking I was 21 at the time and had never had a 'real' boyfriend just a few dates here and there. I watched all the other girls in high school and college with their boyfriends and I would get sad because it wasn't happening for me. I was sitting there getting more and more depressed over the thought that I just began writing my own very long affirmation. "He walked in the room and our eyes caught one another and lit up", and it went on from there. In the end I had affirmed this would happen just the way I wrote it. As I was writing I my mind went somewhere else and I began seeing this whole affirmation in my head as if it were really happening. I saw it all in my head.

After all my writing I took a deep breath and asked my parents who had both passed away by the time I was 21 to please make this happen for me. Honestly I didn't get much work done for the rest of the day; I couldn't get this vision out of my head.

I would read my affirmation over and over for the

next few weeks again seeing it all as if it were happening, it felt good. I would say to my self over and over again, "this will happen". After a few weeks I just let it go and in my mind gave it to my parents and the universe. I no longer thought about it and went on living my daily life working and going to school and watching everyone else with their boyfriends.

A couple of my girlfriends called me one night and asked me if I wanted to go out to a club. I'm not a big club person and hesitated but then decided to go. I met this really good looking guy who was paying attention to me all night but every time I turned around I would see this one guy keep looking at me and I kept looking back. This was one month after writing my affirmation. This went on all night and although I was sitting and talking with the good looking guy this other guy kept grabbing my attention, we just kept looking at each other but we didn't talk. The guy I was talking to asked me for my number and of course never called.

About a week went by and the guy that I had eye contact with all night called me, he had asked one of my friends for my phone number. As we talked on the phone I was realizing he was everything I wrote about in the affirmation. I did however affirm that when I did meet this guy I had in my head we would start dating immediately and we did.

We dated for about six months and he moved in with me and we became engaged months later. I couldn't believe I had a diamond on my finger and a real boyfriend. We did live together for almost three years and most of it was good, we were just finding out we wanted different things in life so we decided to split up. I forgot to affirm that we would stay together forever. I did however get what I did affirm and learned many lessons from this relationship. I gained a confidence I never had and it opened me up to accept relationships into my life because now I had gotten a big taste of what it felt like. I have no regrets. I have learned that affirmations do work and I read and write affirmations all the time now and my life got better because my thinking got better.

"Within you is the divine capacity to manifest and attract all that you need or desire."

Wayne Dyer

Creative Visualization

Ron K, West Palm Beach, FL

I am writing today from the North Shore of Hawaii. My soul mate by my side and together, we are holding hands and enjoying the splendor of nature - the warm sun, the rushing of the waves and of course, the surfers.

No wait; make that a ride on a Gondola in the heart of Venice with the one I love. Make that a mountain summit that we just spent the past three days conquering. We have arrived. Tonight we will spend the evening dining, dancing and having a splendid evening together.

Truth is that I am at my computer in the solitude of my bedroom. Am I crazy for saying that I am doing those other things? No! I am setting my goals through visualization.

I am a goal achiever. I am contacting the inner me and getting in touch with that which I am creating. I have taken the time to use my imagination and create what I want. If I want to be free, I've got to be me!

Through visualization, I am able to create a world that is me. I am able to do this by letting go of the current reality. This process is not only healthy, it is vital to knowing what I want in life. This is how to set goals.

I found that by letting go and imagining that which I want, I can create an image or perhaps a motion picture in my mind. I am able to release all visions of my current reality in order to create a better life. We are, after all, free to be, do or have anything which we desire.

I am also using this process to create my new home and my new car as well as my lifestyle. This helps me to create the images that drive me toward that goal.

Our purpose is to create. When we create we are happy and have purpose. Create or disintegrate! I have formerly lived a destructive life as I allowed the past thoughts and activity to create my current results. This is clearly an example of how recycling is detrimental to the environment. Thoughts are to be fresh and alive as they are a living entity of who we are. The past actions and activity are in the past and do not serve.

I am remembering a quote which states "Faith without works is dead". How can we have faith in something which is not alive? Our past experiences, regardless of how memorable they might be, are dead. We must live in the now. Through the creative process we create the circumstances that move us toward our goals.

We are then driven to action by focusing upon our goals. We have created our purpose through visualizing. The most important thing to remember is that we create our own reality and you do not have to please anyone else, in fact, you really have nothing to offer until you are enjoying you. Others will be attracted to you when you are free.

Success is not a goal. Success is an expression through the realization of who you already are. The beaches, fine restaurants, new cloths or that new car are not success. These things are merely an expression of the success that you have realized in your life. Success can be defined as *"a person who is progressively realizing a worthy ideal"*. This happens by setting those goals and then taking action toward becoming that.

"The important thing is
not to stop questioning."

Albert Einstein

True Abundance

Shawn B.

In life many of us think that we have it all figured out. I was no different. My wife and I thought we had it all, until we started to learn what true abundance and wealth meant.

Shortly after being married and moving away, we learned a few crucial life-lessons. First that we would not make it unless we worked together and second that we did not have it all figured out . . . Especially financially. We managed to rack up over $25,000 in consumer debt in just over two years.

So there we were, just out of college, in debt and confused as to just how we got there.

"At least I have a good job," I thought. "That will always be there to carry us through. . . "

Yeah right! What I thought was my retirement, ended up only being a year long pursuit, that left me even more broke afterwards than before I started.

It wasn't until a chance meeting with a few choice individuals that we started to realize that life was not about "stuff" and the pursuit of more "stuff." Life was about love and laughter, family and friends and the pursuit of happiness, not money. Before work was a means to an end, a means to more and more stuff. After learning proper principles, we were starting to work toward value creation for others as a means to provide for ourselves so that we could spend time with the ones that we loved, sharing in true abundance.

Today my wife and I own and operate several small business endeavors and spend as much time as were learning more and more about what life is really all about.

"There are no miracles for those

who have no faith in them."

French Proverb

Letting Go, Letting God

Jodi R, Georgia

We all have a time in life when the very probable seems impossible. For me it was selling my house. My dream was to move to Georgia for the longest time and I had finally come to grips with moving to another state from NY where I've lived all of my life. The house became unaffordable and we couldn't meet the bills anymore without a struggle as it is very hard to live on Long Island these days. I felt like I was drowning.

My house was on the market for at least 2 years. Day in and day out I'd pray and dwell on selling this house. Eventually we had a buyer for the house. It was nothing but one obstacle after another. After two months of contract dealings etc… the buyer couldn't get the mortgage and the deal fell through.

That was it for me. I resigned myself to the fact that I was supposed to live in NY forever and struggle. It wasn't meant for me to leave and start over. That night I prayed in a way I haven't before, and in addition, cried my eyes out. I became numb.

Instead of begging God to help me sell my house I gave God and The Universe the problem. I said

"You know what's best, but in the meantime I have to live and take care of my life and my children and do what I have to do here, what do I do? I really need and want to sell so I'm leaving it to you." For the first time in my life I truly gave the situation to a higher source.

The next day I went and got a job nothing major just a few hours a day to keep my mind occupied. Started to unpack, repainted the house white and resigned myself to the fact we would have to continue to struggle or lose everything and my hopes for Georgia were gone. I could no longer carry this weight on my shoulders which was the reason I gave the situation to God.

I lived out the real estate contract which expired a month after the deal fell though, August 31. Things were ok. I still wanted to move but I had no bites on the house, but I was ok with that, I had to be. I lived my life and let the house situation take care of itself.

Eventually it did take care of itself. About a week after the real estate contract expired there was a knock on my door at 8am. It was a man who asked my husband if the house was still for sale that he wanted to buy it. He remembered the sign that was there before the real estate took it down. My husband told him if he was serious to come back with his wife at a reasonable time and we'll show him the house and gave him our phone number.

Without any more thought to that because we figured it was just another looker we went through our daily routines as normal. That evening the man called and came to look at the house with his wife. Needless to say they loved it and wanted to buy it and they did. They had more than an ample amount of money to put down and get a mortgage and we closed within a month in half. In NY State a month and a half is fast.

So this is my story of how letting go and leaving things up to God or the universe is what we need to do. Everything will be taken care of when the time is right. The best thing that happened to me was that my house was sold without a realtor. I didn't have to pay an $18,000 real estate fee. It was worth the wait. I moved out of state I've been gone over a year now. I got want I wanted and what I felt me and my family needed. No regrets. God and The Universe took care of me when needed and they will take care of me again, I've seen for myself what letting go can do for your life. It allows you to move forward and progress.

"To one who has faith,
no explanation is necessary.
To one without faith,
no explanation is possible."

St. Thomas Aquinas

St. Jude Answered My Prayer

Annette C, North Carolina

I was in a mentally abusive relationship for a couple of years when I decided to leave. I was also previously married and that ended in divorce. I began dating and it was one disaster after the next. Needless to say I was very lonely and the television became my best friend.

I worked day and night at two separate jobs to make ends meet; I was exhausted by the end of the day. I knew this was no way to live but didn't have a choice. I have to admit I wasn't happy with my life but never ever allowed anyone to see my unhappiness. I tried by myself to treat myself the best way I could and act like the Goddess God intended me to be after all I was all I had.

I prayed to St. Jude religiously every single night to bring me the right partner. It was hard at first but figured I'd give it a try. As time went on it became easier and easier to pray to him and I kept asking for the same thing over and over and started to believe he was going to help me. Over the next year I could say that myself and St. Jude became best friends, I felt him on my side and believed he was working on my behalf.

I was alone for the next year and continued my daily routine, no dates, no love life. My marriage and my relationship were so bad that I felt like I was always alone. I wanted it to be different this time and as time went on my faith in St. Jude grew.

One day after leaving work I had went to open the door and at the same exact time this man went to open the door and our hands touched. We laughed about it and then went into a nice conversation. We enjoyed our conversation so much that he asked me if I would like to go have dinner and I accepted. It was wonderful and we began dating. He was everything I had asked St. Jude for.

One year later we were engaged. He gave me the most beautiful ring that it brought tears to my eyes because I had never experienced this. A year later we were married in a lavish wedding, a wedding I could have never dreamed of. Everything was beautiful and I was finally happy.

As a bonus he told me to quit one of my jobs because he didn't want me to work so hard, so I did. Today we are happily married, live in a beautiful home and travel a lot which is another thing I never really did. St. Jude answered my prayers in such a way I could have never imagined. Thank you St. Jude!

"My philosophy is that not only
are you responsible for your life,
but doing the best at this moment
puts you in the best place
for the next moment."

Oprah Winfrey

Visualized Prosperity

Frank B, Elizabethtown PA

My wife was always into visualizing what she wanted and would tell me about things she visualized for that came to be. I never really got into that type of thing so I would just listen. We were in financial trouble at the time and it looked like the next couple of months were going to be shaky. I don't know what came over me but I went to her and asked her to visualize money coming to us after all it seemed to work for the things she wanted so I figured it wouldn't hurt.

Just the very next day I got a call from Ford Motor Company telling me I had excellent credit with them and they were offering us a month free, no car payment. With the payment being $300 per month that was a huge help. I still wasn't sure if this was because my wife visualized more money, but I was happy about that phone call to say the least.

I had told my wife not to cook that night and that we would take the kids and go out to eat to celebrate the phone call, no place fancy just out to eat at the pizzeria so we went. Everyone told me what they wanted and I went and ordered the food. They brought the food to the table and we had our dinner.

I went up to pay after we were done and they had told me I already paid. I knew I didn't pay and told them they made a mistake assuming they would figure it out anyway and they insisted I paid. I went over and asked my wife if she had paid and she said she didn't. I went up again and told them there was a mistake that we didn't pay and again they insisted I did. I wasn't going to stand there all night and argue this so I said thank you and left. The free meal was delicious and I couldn't get over the fact that they really thought I paid because I was only dealing with one person.

Two days later my wife opened up the mail and there was a check for $800 in the envelope from my union claiming it was money they owed me for something, something I didn't even know about or expect. Within 3 days we received what summed up to be $1100 plus a free meal.

My wife claims it was because she visualized the whole thing not in those details but visualized extra money. It made me a believer.

"We judge a man's wisdom by his hope."

Ralph Waldo Emerson

Touched By an Angel

Lori B, Oregon

This story changed my life almost three years ago.

My best Friend Angela passed away on Sept 4, 2004. I lay next to her and heard her heart beat for the last time, and as it did I died inside with her.

Six months prior she was told by her Doctors she had a very rare form of Cancer and was giving only ninety days to live with no hope for a cure just to make her peace and die. Now Angel (Angela) was a very spiritual person, she use to tell me if I didn't change my ways that I was going to go to Hell, I disagreed.

Many years of listening to her wisdom I began to rebuild my relationship with God. I tried to not do the things I new were wrong and prayed, and my life got a little less complicated. But I am a weak soul and got back into old pity party habits, and lost focus on my salvation, got with the wrong people, walked along side the devil himself once again, started using meth to numb my deep seeded inner pain, and didn't know how to release all the hurt, hate, sadness, I had been carrying around since a young girl.

When Angel told me she was dying I blamed myself, see I believe that all your wrong doings will come back to you some way or another, usually on something or someone who is innocent.

I lost my two beautiful daughters, my house, my cars, my money, and my soul, and now I would once again lose one of only two people who truly showed me unconditional love, (my Brother was the first he past away in 1983). How do I go on? Well, I put a good act.

Angel asked me to be with her and help take care of her. I did spend every day and night talking, laughing, crying, praying, and wishing for a miracle. I put every ounce of energy I had in rebuilding my relationship with God, Angel and my kids, but lied every step of the way, continued using drugs and drinking to numb my self and thought it would all be ok.

Sept 4th came and at 11:36 am time stopped for me. I managed to get strength, her body was not removed until 5am and I comforted every one, brushed her hair, painted her toes and kept on wishing that she would open her eyes, smile with that smile that lit my soul, but she didn't. We buried her on Friday the 10th of Sept. I played the role good. I never shed a tear in front of anyone, but was screaming with agony inside.

I sat there on the 11th and I broke. I took a bottle of her morphine, swallowed about 49 pills and laid down where she died and said "I'm coming to be with you my angel". I woke up the next morning pills in my hand and her presence all around, (goose bumps still go through me when I think of it) I cant explain why, what, how. I was alone no one knew of my intentions. I can only say that an Angel saved my soul that day, and gave me the power and strength to truly forgive myself and forgive all the ones who helped me get there. I went to church that morning and my Pastor was preaching on the power of Gods love and forgiveness and to be reborn. He was speaking to about one hundred or more people there but his words where pondered into me. I was baptized that day; I began a new life is it perfect? No. Do I still sin? Of course, but I am aware of my actions and no more *poor pity parties* for me.

Its been almost three years now and it has not been easy, I struggle more some days than others, I have began to rebuild my relations with my gifts from God, my girls. Daphne now 21 and married has forgiven me. We are getting close again. Jasmyn who will be 15 on May 28th, is my continued reason to be a better person every day, she is slowly connecting with me. I hurt her so bad that she was very confused and scared to trust me again, I don't blame her I did a very unforgiving thing. I thought throwing your self away is one thing but throwing the gifts God gave me away (my daughters), never.

Everything is forgivable; it just needs time to heal.

I never regret my past; it is what made me today. I love myself, love life and try to be the best I can be. I thank God for sending me an Angel to show me the path I always knew was there but had no courage to walk that curved road.

I love her and always will. She never left me nor my brother, they had a job to do and that job I believe is me.

I am a survivor of child molestation, and spent many years of punishing myself for things I had no control over. Forgiveness is such a beautiful thing and so easy. I have accepted the wrongs in my life and only try to wake up every new day and see what new thing I will learn that day. My past is my past, my future is mine. Courage, Strength, power, and wisdom are my goals.

"Your are the writer, director
and producer of your life.
You can make it a great adventure!"

Bruce Goldwell

Positive Thinking, Affirmations and Faith Give New Purpose

Traci B, Michigan

I am a 36 year old wife and mother of 3 beautiful children. My life is happy and peaceful, but it hasn't always been this way.

As a child my father was an alcoholic and beat my mother on a regular basis, of course I would always jump in to try and stop the abuse. Sometimes it worked, sometimes it didn't. I always went to bed afraid to sleep in case my dad started to beat my mom again.

In addition to that, my uncle molested me from the time I was in diapers until I was 11 years old. His famous words for what he was doing was "this is what boys are going to do to you when you get older", wow, what a nice thing to do to a child and to tell a child.

Eventually in 1981 my mother divorced my father and my uncle enlisted in the navy. I thought things were going to be wonderful, I couldn't be any more wrong. After the divorce my mom decided that she didn't have kids anymore. She ran around constantly drinking and doing drugs and left me home alone to take care of my younger sister. Sometimes she was gone for days, sometimes weeks. Eventually she would come back and when she would it was no cake walk for me. I was constantly put down and called all kinds of filthy names, when she was really drunk I was beaten. Sometimes it was with her fists, sometimes a broom stick, sometimes a belt, but her favorite was a piece of the garden hose that she had cut off. Believe me; she did not care where she hit me either.

Finally at 16 and a-half years old I moved out of my house and in with a friend of mine and her mom. I finished high school and went on to business school.

I ended up quitting because the "demons" of my past wouldn't leave me alone. I turned to drinking for a while, drugs for a while, none of which eased the pain at all.

When I was 21 years old I woke up one day and said, "enough is enough", I do not want to be my mom, I do not want to be my dad", then and there I decided my life had to change. How did I turn my life around you ask? By the power of positive thinking and the use of affirmations! For those of you who don't know what affirmations are, they are positive statements said and/or written with the intent of what you want from your life. One of the main ones I used and still use to this day is: "I deserve to be happy".

You see I was very self destructive for a very long time. Every time things were going good in my life I felt I didn't deserve that, I felt that things were supposed to be chaotic so I would start to think negative and ruin whatever was going good. This was not acceptable. I decided to turn my negatives into positives. Every time a negative would come into my mind I would say to myself "stop" and turn the negative around. Example: "you are doing nothing with your life", I would then say "I work very hard for my children, I am a good mom, a good wife, I am doing a lot with my life".

In addition, I would pray every night to God and a Goddess (I believe that all gods are one god) and ask for their help and interception with my "demons" in my mind. Thankfully between them granting my prayers, the miracle of positive thinking and the help of affirmations I was able to turn my life around.

This was very difficult at first, but as the years went on it got much easier. Do the "demons" try and rear their ugly little heads every now and then? Yes they do. But I do not allow them to stay for very long. I turn it over, get back to being positive and all ends well.

"It is this belief in a power larger than myself
and other than myself,
which allows me to venture into the
unknown and even the unknowable."

Maya Angelou

Strength, Faith and Affirmations

Traci B, Michigan

I am a survivor of mental, physical and sexual abuse.

As a result of the abuse I developed an anxiety disorder with agoraphobia as well as severe depression. For those of you who do not know what agoraphobia is - this is the fear of basically everything. People who are agoraphobic do not want to suffer panic attacks and retreat to the safety of their own homes and become "house bound".

Back in 1990 my mother, who was one of my abusers passed away. After her death I started having panic attacks by 1991 I was agoraphobic and house bound.

I did not leave my house for almost a year! I wouldn't even go on the front porch to get the mail out of the mail box. Eventually the panic attacks started happening at home and there was "no where left to hide".

Since I was a "prisoner of my own mind and my own house" something had to be done. I relied on the power of my faith and the strength I had in me as a survivor and decided I had to venture out into the "scary world". I started doing "baby steps" going out front, eventually moving to walking around the block, then going to stores and finally driving again. I did a lot of talking to myself, telling myself "I can do it" and I did for quite sometime. Until 1996, the anxiety came back in full force. It got so bad I became depressed and suicidal. I had to stay alive for my son so I decided to check myself into the hospital. I stayed there for 7 nights and 8 days and was put on medication. A lot of people out there suffering with these disorders feel that getting on medication makes you weak, that's what I thought to, until I was put on them. I learned it doesn't make you weak; it takes a stronger person to get help. If I had high blood pressure and needed medication I would take it without a second thought, well, it's the same for my anxiety and depression meds. I need them, I take them.

But medication alone did not get me through this situation. I turned to my faith, I wrote affirmations daily, such as: "I can go anywhere, anytime with comfort and ease", I paid attention to what I said to myself and turned negatives into positives, I also found that progressive relaxation and deep breathing was a huge help for me.

Anxiety and depression is very scary, sometimes you feel helpless, sometimes you feel hopeless and sometimes you just feel plain crazy. I learned through the various techniques above that I can manage my anxiety and depression and live my life. Is it easy? No.

Do I still have "bad days"? Yes. But when I do, I turn to my higher power, I write my affirmations, I talk positively to myself, I do my relaxation and I don't fight the fear.

I went from a woman who couldn't leave her home to a woman who started facilitating at a support group for people with anxiety and depression, a mom who is very involved with her children and their schools, and a woman who even when anxious I go out and do things anyway. I refuse to let my past, my abuse, my fears, my anxiety and my depression to ever take hold of my life again and make me lose who I am.

If you are suffering from anxiety and depression, know that you are not alone and that you can over come.

"Nothing is too good to be true,
nothing is too wonderful to happen,
nothing is too good to last;
when you look to the *"Infinite Spirit"*
for your good."

Florence Scovel Shinn

The Luck of the Ladybug

Charlene P, NY

I've always believed in the luck of ladybugs, sounds strange I know. I was taught while very young that ladybugs bring good luck.

There were many times I needed a ladybug to land upon me but they never did. I would see them land on other people but never me.

I was a single mom struggling for everything I had. With a job that didn't pay well everything was a struggle. I had no one special in my life while everyone I knew was in love and having good relationships, I felt hopeless.

Night after night I cried and cried and prayed for things to get better. Things were getting worse as I was waiting for them to get better. How could I enjoy anything with the fear of losing everything and no one to share my burdens with?

I searched for a better job with more income but because of my daughters hours at school it was hard. I couldn't afford a babysitter or day care so I just felt stuck. It was a truly horrible time and a single mom's worst nightmare.

A friend of mine, a very good friend was planning on taking a trip to Salem, MA. She had told me she had gone there once before and it seemed like such a magical place. When she told me about the trip I was in awe wishing I could go as well. She had called me a few days later and asked me if I would like to go. Since she was driving and getting a hotel room anyway she said it really wouldn't cost me anything and felt I needed to get away. I of course was excited over this.

In April we had went on the trip. It was beautiful there. There were so many interesting people to talk to as well. I spoke with a few people there as well about my belief in the luck of the ladybug and to my surprise they had all heard of it. We took a walk by the water and for a few minutes I just sat by myself and begged God to give me a sign that things would get better in my life.

While we were there my friend treated me to a psychic reading, I was hoping to hear some good news. What I heard was what was exactly happening in my life but that things would become better if I just believed they would. She advised me to go home and write out how I wanted my life to be and to try my hardest to believe that dreams do come true. I went back to the hotel that night and wrote like she had said to do and with conviction.

We stayed there for a few days and then came home, what a beautiful place.

I kept reading what I wrote over and over to try and get it to all sink into my brain. I went on with my daily life as it was.

The next month a neighbor who lived across the street from me called me on the phone and told me to look at my front door which of course I thought was a strange request but I did. To my total delight my front door had ladybugs all over it. I had never seen so many ladybugs; there were enough for my neighbor to see them from across the street. I was amazed. Some actually flew in but I didn't care, I let them in hoping they were bringing the luck I had always heard about with them.

It was about a month later I had run into an old friend and we began talking. She told me of a place she was working at and told me they were hiring. The hours were perfect since those were the hours my daughter was in school. I went for the interview and got the job, a good paying job with benefits. My neighbor had told me that when my daughter was off from school for holidays and vacations that se would gladly watch her. I was ecstatic.

I began working and loved the job. The money was enough to cover everything and leave us some extra for pleasure. To my surprise I had met a very nice man there and we've been on a few dates. It's not a relationship but it felt good to be dating again and to feel wanted.

I believe something magical happened when I went away with my friend. What that magic is I don't know, I'll never know but whatever it was the ladybugs charged to my door and brought me the luck I always believed they would bring. My advice to anyone reading this is that when a ladybug lands on you or flies into your home, expect something good to happen.

"Sometimes the Universe doesn't give us exactly what we want when we want it, because there's actually something better down the road."

Anonymous

A Butterfly from Heaven

Grace L, Ephrata PA

After my mom had died two years ago my husband decided to leave me for another woman. I was very upset of course but I did see the end coming as we were not getting along for the longest time. What I didn't know was how very hard it would be to live on my own with my kids.

I sold basically everything we had and started over. Between my mom's death and the ending of my marriage I felt I needed a new start. I bought new things with the money I had gotten from selling what I had and of course adding more to it. As bad as my marriage was getting I did however feel lonely. I heard the dating scene was horrible and boy did I find out quick that it was. I gave up on dating for awhile and took the advice of a friend to have some alone time.

Night after night after the kids were asleep it was me and the VCR. Night after night I felt more and more lonely. My loneliness grew so much that I would just break down and cry and wish for someone to come into my life. I hadn't had affection for a long time even though I was married. There wasn't any affection in the marriage but for some reason I didn't feel lonely then, I guess I was in denial.

The year after my mom died I read every life after death book there was. My main concern in reading them was the signs your loved ones give you. I had gotten quite a few when she first passed but then they went away. Strangely enough I got them before my marriage broke up. Was she trying to tell me something?

I was sitting outside one day trying to collect my thoughts on how I was going to put my life back together when this beautiful butterfly kept flying around my head. I tried swooshing him away but he wouldn't leave since I really don't like bugs. Then I remembered something I had read after mom passed. I read that butterflies are a sign that a loved one is around you, that their there to comfort you. It had something to do with the metamorphic life of a butterfly. I stopped swooshing him away, he wasn't leaving anyway. He then landed on my knee and just stayed there. I felt such peace with this bug on my knee. At that point I didn't see him as a bug I saw him as a sign from mom. I wondered what he was there to tell me. He stayed for awhile, quite awhile and then left. The butterfly left me with such a peaceful feeling, a feeling I cannot explain. I then put the radio on and I kept hearing all these very deep love songs. I remembered yet another thing I had read in that book. It was when a loved one passes and you want a sign from them say a quick prayer for a sign and turn on the radio since they also come to you through any source of energy. It made sense to me because they are in fact a form of energy now. Although I didn't say a prayer mom was heavily on my mind after the butterfly landed on me. In my heart at that moment I knew something good was coming, I didn't know when but I knew it was coming.

A few months later my friend had introduced me to a single male friend of hers. We took a liking to one another and began to see one another on a regular basis. It's been a year now that were together and I've never been so happy. I have all the affection I could ever need.

Thank you pretty butterfly!

Thank you mom!

"During our lives we all wish to be in a certain place, be with a certain person, and have certain things that we think will make us happy, when in fact God already knows what's best for us and in the end we come to understand his plan."

Deborah Buchanan

God Heard My Plea

Robert E., Lafayette, La.

It was after my second year in law school. Came home, didn't have a job lined up. I was really depressed, just lying on my bed. Finally got to the point where I simply said "God help me." Well, about a minute later there was a knock on the door.

It was a friend I hadn't seen in a while. He was driving by and saw my car. He asked if I wanted to take a drive to a town about 20 miles south of here. I said "sure". On the way we stop at the store. I see two fraternity brothers (alumni) who worked at a law firm. They asked me about school and I told them my grades. One of them was in charge of hiring and said to come by on the following Monday. Well yes, I got the job, clerked there the remainder of the summer. Then I arranged my schedule to be able to commute and worked there the beginning of my last year. Got a job offer and I am still with that same firm 24 years later.

I guess that is why I have stayed there through thick and thin passing up other opportunities. Always figured it was the place I needed and was destined to be. The coincidences were too much of a direct heartfelt answer to a plaintive plea to be anything other than a direct answer to prayer and a willingness on the part of every piece of the Universal God force to assist.

"*The Universe* is always at work.
Not only does it respond to our desires when
faith and belief are strong enough
but perhaps responds to our needs first.
The mind tends to think and feel more for
our needs. The *Universe* knows of our needs
before we convey them."

Deborah Buchanan

The Universe Manifested Her Need

Sydney C, NY

I manifested 33 dollars in 4 days. Yes I did! It was right after Christmas 2006 and I of course had spent all of my dollars on Christmas. I was staying at my son's home and I hadn't enough money to get the subway and get home. Well I read about this site in a yahoo group I belong to. I figured, well why not, I'll try it.

The beginning of the exercise is to manifest one dollar first. I figured that would be easy to do since I knew I was capable of at least bringing in one dollar into my reality. I did the exercise for four days. I was real easy about it. I didn't even really concern myself with how it was going to show up besides it was just one dollar. I wanted to play the game with integrity so I did not ask my son for any money. Besides he always gives me that look if I do.

So each day I did the exercise suggested. As I was packing up to leave my sons house to catch the subway, he unprompted by me hands me 13 dollars for a cab ride home and an extra 20 bucks. WooHoo! How delicious!! From 12/26/06 to 12/30/06, I manifested 33 dollars.

"Infinite Spirit,
Open the way for my great abundance.
I am an irresistible magnet for all that
belongs to me by *"Divine Right"*.

Florence Scovel Shinn

Good Karma and Poetry

Vickie W., Tooele, Utah

While at a women's shelter for battered women, I was approached to go before the Utah congress to try to better the laws to help battered women. I had to speak, it was very scary for me, but I did it and we got some tougher laws passed here in Utah.

Then in 1991 myself and my two children, then 7 and 3, became part of the homeless. While we were at the family shelter in Salt Lake City, the director decided to run a series of profiles on the homeless, my children and I were picked.

I am very proud that I could help enlighten people's minds to the plight of the homeless. I now look at them in totally different light.

I now own my own home and when my two little sisters, faced becoming homeless, I took them in, I couldn't help all of the others out there on the street, but I could do this one small thing.

I have written poetry my whole life, starting at the age of 19 as a healing process.

It's no wonder Stevie Nicks song, *"Street Angel"* means so much to me. My maiden name happens to be 'Street'.

"Yesterday is but a dream,
and tomorrow is only a vision,
but today well lived makes every yesterday a
dream of happiness and
every tomorrow a vision of hope."

Anonymous

Courage and the Law of Attraction

G. L. Giles, Summerville, SC

I was introduced to the Law of Attraction, via The Secret, in April 2006. I was definitely attracting it into my life because I'd finally let go of some of my old baggage and allowed what I really wanted to manifest.

Three days after I watched The Secret, I gave my two weeks notice at a job that I didn't want to be working at, and I started pursuing my writing career in earn-est (my different spelling to prove a point: I was to start making a living, earning $$$, at what I really loved doing). I started reading everything I could get my hands on regarding the Law of Attraction and Quantum Physics. This began what I call my "Quantum Mechanical Quest." I followed what Bob Proctor said to do in the "Bob Proctor's Secret Summary" part of The Secret. So, I studied other "switched on" teachers' writings, DVDs, cds, etc. in great depth. For instance, I've been doing Bill Harris' *Holosync* program for nine months now, and watching numerous James Ray DVDs, etc. I also had the good fortune to meet him and have my picture taken with him (because I intended it) in Greenville, SC at one of his conferences in May 2007.

Ah, the positive power in concentrating on what I wanted versus what I didn't want. A great example of this lies in the fact that even though I'm a self-published author, I haven't let it stop me from getting in major bookstores. Before the knowledge of the Law of Attraction in April 2006, I hadn't been in even one major bookstore to have a signing. I used to think thoughts like, *"How will I ever get into a major bookstore when I'm just self-published, and I'm not as talented as the other legitimate non-self-published authors."* I had to flip that switch and work on changing my negative self-defeatist inner talk to positive I-can-do-it, I don't know how but I know what I want, inner and outer talk. And it worked!!

My book is now on the shelves in five states (South Carolina, North Carolina, Georgia, Alabama and Florida). And I've had over eighty book signing events at since my first signing in September of 2006. Furthermore, I have a weekly podcast with my friend Bobbyjo where we talk about the Law of Attraction, Quantum Physics, great books to read we've already had over 3,000 downloads since our first *ChiQchat* podcast episode was published the end of February 2007.

I am so happy and grateful that I followed my heart and my dream.

"You gain strength, courage, and confidence by every experience in which you really stop to look fear in the face."

Eleanor Roosevelt

All Situations End Up As They Were Meant To Be

Robert E., Lafayette, La.

I was just thinking one night how it would be nice to have a nice companion - a woman very beautiful and attractive to me. Someone who was interested in what I was working on spiritually. The next morning I go to the Health Club and there is a guy I know walking with a very attractive woman. I said "hi" and went on about my business.

I went out later that night and that same woman waves me over. She asks my name. I told her my name. Then she says that she had tried to send me an email but I never responded. Long story but I met a friend of hers at an out of state airport who lived around here. Her friend said she knew someone who would be perfect for me and asked me for my email address.

Never heard anything and forgot about it. Turns out the woman did try to email me. But our firm's email filter didn't let her email go through.

I figured out the reason I didn't get her email. At first she didn't believe me, but then she did. We went out the following Friday and that began a two week very serious relationship. And at the time I was thinking *"Ask and it is Given"*

Well, the "serious relationship" became more time consuming and complicated than I desired. I didn't want to hurt her feelings, so I asked God to work it out and let the relationship unwind gently.

That night she gets a call from her former boyfriend. He is saying what a "dumb..." he was and he wanted her back. She called all confused. I told her I would bow out of the equation to avoid any complications and told her to work out her situation.

Well two for two. Start and stop in perfect divine order. She wanted someone who could make a commitment to her and I was the person who helped her get what she wanted - not from me - from the other boyfriend. They are still together and it is as it should be.

"There is a divine reason for all the people
we meet on our path. Some stay.
Some go. We may never know the reason
why. Who are we to question a power
greater than ourselves?"

Deborah Buchanan

A Destined Meeting

Jodi R., Georgia

It's been around 13 years now that I met who I consider my best friend and perhaps my soul-mates.

I was a soccer coach at the time and her son played on my team although I had never met her, it was the start of the season. I had turned around and saw a man with whom my husband had went to school with and was very good friends with back then. I was happy to see him and knew my husband would be as well. During the years they had lost touch. As it turned out his son played on my team which is the reason he was there. We talked for awhile and laughed about old times.

All of a sudden this woman had walked over onto the field and went and stood by this man. He introduced her to me as his wife. I was wearing tiny sun glasses at the time with yes, peace signs on them and she commented that she liked my glasses at which point for some reason I knew we would get along.

I invited them to come over after the game and they did. Of course the husbands went outside to catch up and we stayed inside and talked. It turned out we had almost everything in common, it was strange. We exchanged numbers and talked on the phone all the time and as couples got together at least once a week. Our husbands talked and laughed while we were together but you could see that their connection wasn't there anymore. We on the other hand were becoming closer and closer. She told me everything and I told her everything. Strange but it was if we were the same people but in different bodies.

About a year later her and her husband split up and she was devastated mainly because she didn't expect it. Her husband had come to me a few times to talk but it was her I wanted to be there for. As in all marital separations there were certain people calling me to bad mouth her, people who really had some nerve knowing what I now know and I just felt it was very evil but people can be that way, they will kick you when your down, usually that goes back to them one day. I had to laugh though because I knew of things these certain people would have never wanted me to know but as I said her and I told each other everything! I would have no part of this ridiculous gossip. The way I saw it was that she was good to these people and they were stabbing her in the back, I wasn't having any part of it. My concern was helping her through this rough time.

For what would be the next ten years it was me and her. Of course I had a family to tend to but we were becoming closer and closer and everyone began to take notice of the similarities. Everywhere and I mean everywhere we went people thought we were sisters and we don't look alike. People never even told me that about my own sisters and I. Did they sense something we didn't know?

I believe in the after-life and I truly believed I knew her in another place and time. We spoke alike, we said the same things at the same time and we thought alike, I could read her mind just by looking at her. I knew her better than anyone.

The relationship lasts until this day even though I moved away. We would tend to go through spurts were we wouldn't speak for awhile only due to things that were going on with our lives but then we'd pick up as if no time had passed with no questions. It's to the point were she can email me one word and I already know the whole story and the same with me. I've never had a connection like this with a friend.

We've gone through so much together, more than some people go through in a lifetime and the memories are endless and always funny since she's one of the funniest people I've ever met. She claims I crack her up as well but I tend to be a little more serious.

To make the story stranger, I had known her mother for years before I met her. Her mother was everyone's favorite bartender and I was close with her for years before meeting her daughter. Stranger was that I was just like her mother and she was just like my mother. This connection never ceased to amaze me it got stranger and stranger. The relationship is still strong through the good and the bad.

I definitely believe and always will believe that I knew her in another lifetime, nothing else could explain it, and it was just a matter of time before the universe put us back together.

"Life can be a struggle at times,
but then there are those times,
when a true miracle enters our life.
Life is full of surprises."

Deborah Buchanan

Miracles Do Happen

Kathleen M., Salt Lake City, Utah

Back in 1999, I went to the doctor for a physical as I did every year, the doctor decided to do some blood tests because I had not been feeling very well for quite some time. Well a few days later I got a call from the doctor telling me I needed to come in. Right then I knew something bad was wrong I thought maybe my cancer had come back which I was diagnosed with in 1989. So I made an appointment to go in when I got there the doctor told me to sit down needless to say I freaked thinking *"here we go again."* Yes I was scared very scared.

He then told me I had Hepatitis C at that time I had no idea what Hep C was I had never heard of it before I asked him just *"what is Hep C?"* He said it was a liver disease and it was also in my blood. I asked him is that really bad he said there is no cure for it but didn't tell me much more than that. So I figured well it must not be too bad.

When I went home I got on the internet and looked up Hepatitis C, I read all about it that is when I realized I was handed a death sentence. For the few months I went into a deep depression thinking what the hell is there to live for. I even tried to commit suicide. My friend found me and called 911. I woke up 3 days later. The doctor said I was comatose for 3 days and died 3 times. I asked him. *"Why did you bring me back to life I don't want to live?"* He asked me why? I said *"I have Hep C and there's no cure".* He told me you can still live a long life if you take care of yourself. I told him *"but I'm so sick all the time I don't want to live like this".*

When I got released from the hospital I started to do a lot of thinking about what I had just done and how stupid I was because you see I'm not a quitter. This is when I decided to turn it all around I learned about different herbs and things for Hep C and started taking lots of different ones they did help a lot but I was still very sick so I told my self "there has to be another way".

This is when I turned to GOD even though I wasn't sure he was real. I knew there was a higher power. I just wasn't sure it was GOD. Anyways I began to pray a lot and had a lot of people praying for me also.

Well nothing for years but I didn't give up I just kept on praying at this point I didn't really want to die but it was so hard because I was so very sick I couldn't really do anything for myself I couldn't eat or anything. I had had no one to help me because my family was stuck in there own little worlds they just didn't have time for me so I went through all this alone. Needless to say I lost all my so called friends, they didn't want to deal with a sick person so for many years I pretty much was all alone. I couldn't go anywhere I was too sick and had no strength or energy. Most of the time I just slept a lot the doctor put me on Interferon which made me even sicker it was very nasty stuff. I could only take it for three months of the 48 because my white blood count kept going too low and they couldn't get it to come back up so they took me off of it but I never gave up praying.

The doctor sent me for an ultra sound on my liver my brother Randy went with me because I don't drive. He was sitting next to me watching when all of a sudden he popped up and said *"you guys are not going to believe me but I just saw a perfect face of Jesus in your liver"*. I knew right then something was happening, the lady that did the ultra sound left. When she came back she had this big smile on her face she said *"I can't really give you the results but I can say you have nothing to worry about"*. We left.

Within three days the doctor called me back and told me to come in. When I got there he was reading the results of the ultra sound. He just kept on saying *"oh my GOD,"oh my GOD"* and smiling, he said *"your*

Hep C is gone and not only that but you have a brand new liver". He said "*I don't understand how that could happen with all the scarring you had on your liver*". He said "it's all goneeeeeeeeeeeeeee". He said "*that's impossible*", I looked at him and said "*not with GOD nothing is impossible with GOD*". He told me "*you really are a true miracle*". He said "*it will never come back again*". I said "*I know*". Needless to say it made him a believer. Praise The Lord!

I have now been Hep C free for almost 2 years now in September this year. PRAISEEEEEEEEEEE THE LORD! He's so awesome. If you're not a believer, trust me he is real and I'm living proof.

"Practice faith,
expect a miracle."

Deborah Buchanan

Debbie's Corner for Meditative Thought

Debbie Buchanan

Suggestions for Personal and Inspirational Growth

Bring yourself into a relaxed mood and sit and write down all the good you've accomplished in your life, whether it is things you've done to improve your own life or the life of another. Feel the achievement, the good karma and then go and reward yourself for a job well done. Not only will this lift your confidence but allow you to feel complete joy in what you've accomplished.

"Today I appreciate myself"

~~~

We all need some sort of sacred space which usually is our home. A place where you can go and sit down take a deep breath and visualize, pray, speak with and honor your loved ones and just send your dreams out into the *Universe*. Make yourself a prayer stand or personal altar. You don't need much space to make one, you can use a small table, a bookshelf, or whatever suits you. Arrange some candles and incense on it and whatever feels personal to you. They should be items and pictures that make you feel relaxed and tranquil. For example: crystals, sea shells, pictures of loved ones, any religious articles, affirmation cards or statues that mean something to you. You can drape your altar with a beautiful scarf or tablecloth, again anything that means something to you as this will become your personal space. Sit there, relax and allow the *Universe* to take over.

"It is here that I send my thoughts out"

~~~

So much has been said about the written word. There's power in what we write. We can write our life's script. Buy yourself a beautiful journal or just use a regular notebook and begin writing. Write your dreams in the tense that it's already happened, there is a magic to that. Visualize all of the details, write in detail. Light a candle, relax and just write away. It's amazing the dreams we sometimes never realize that we have. Dream! Write! Believe in what your writing that yes, this can happen. One very important factor in this is to, *be careful what you wish for.*

"Today I begin writing my life story"

~~~

You spend most of your time doing good things for

others, why don't you decide now to do something nice for yourself?

- Treat yourself to a beautiful bouquet of flowers.
- Indulge yourself with a large scooped ice cream cone.
- Light candles and step into a bath filled with your favorite essential oils, relax and allow yourself to go to places you've never been to before.
- Slip into cozy PJ's and watch your favorite movies all night.
- Don't cook, order out and eat by candlelight.
- Listen to beautiful music that takes you back to happy memories.
- Relax and read an inspiring book.
- Do whatever makes you happy and comfortable, but remember right now it's all about you because you matter.

"Today belongs to me"

~~~

Begin your own personal journal. There are so many different and unique ways to keep a journal. You can of course keep a daily journal on how your day went and your feelings about the events of that day.

You can keep a journal on special occasions so you'll remember every moment of that special day and hand it down generation after generation. A holiday journal is also a nice idea, it will remind generations to come of your special traditions. A nice way to see how your changing and growing is to keep an 'About Me' journal in which you would write about all the things you love and your views on different topics. When you look back you'll see how much you've grown over the years. Many people love quotes and poetry, why not buy a beautiful journal book and write all your favorite quotes and poems to leave out for everyone to read, it's also a beautiful way to express yourself in a unique way and can be a great 'pick me up' on days when you need to read something of a positive nature. There's so many beautifully decorated journals on the market, why not choose one and begin expressing who you are and the wonderful events of your life and the wonderful person you are. The different ways to journal are countless. Journaling can turn into a wonderful expressive hobby.

"Today I begin to express who I really am".

~~~

We've all read articles that we'd like to keep, came across photos of famous people we admire, clippings out of a newspaper of events we'd like to read back on one day. Keeping a scrapbook is a wonderful way to do that. There are aisles and aisles of scrap booking materials in the craft stores but I'm talking about just an old fashioned scrapbook. It can be the type of scrapbook where in time the pages yellow and so do the pictures and articles. There's something timeless to that look. Keeping a scrapbook is a wonderful hobby. You can collect pictures of your favorite celebrity, cut out articles of world events and articles you may have read that inspired you in some way that you'd love to read over and over again. There's countless ways to keep a scrapbook and it turns into a fun and rewarding hobby that will constantly keep you on the look out. Another great scrapbook to keep is one on yourself; awards you've received, beautiful letters people have written to you, even ticket stubs to a concert or play you've seen. You can allow your imagination run away with all the different things you can keep a scrapbook on. It's a wonderful way to keep busy on those rainy days and build memories for years to come.

"Today I begin a hobby that will bring me pleasure in years to come"

~~~

You don't have to wait till New Years to begin a new resolution. What is it in your life that you want to change that will make you a better person, give you better health, and bring you more loving and lasting relationships and friendships, and/or help you to serve others in a more abundant way. A good way to do this is to get the *"Mastery of New Life Resolutions"* which has affirmations that will help you to stay on tract. You can keep track of what happens each day of your life for 365 days and the personal thoughts and feelings that you have. Over 50% of people who begin New Years resolutions before half the year is through. *"Mastery of New Life Resolutions"* is a support tool that can help you stay on track and see how your life is improving on a daily basis. There is no better time then right now to begin to have more abundant health, wealth and love. Decide what you want to change and start your New Life Resolution now.

"I begin right now to create my new life
resolutions
so I can have greater
health, wealth and love!"

Bruce Goldwell

"Four steps forward and two steps back - is still two steps forward."

Robert Ellender

"There is a valid reason for everything that happens. We usually don't realize it until well after the event takes place, but looking back it is all part of a grand cosmic scheme."

Robert Ellender

"I don't know how, I just know I will."

Bruce Goldwell

"No problem can be solved from the same consciousness that created it. We must learn to see the world anew."

Albert Einstein

Diary of Thoughts

Date_____

_____

_____

_____

_____

_____

Date_____

_____

_____

_____

_____

_____

Date_____

_____

_____

_____

_____

_____

Date_____

_____

_____

_____

_____

_____

Date_____

_____

_____

_____

_____

_____

Date_____

_____

_____

_____

_____

_____

Date_____

_____

_____

_____

_____

_____

Date_____

_____

_____

_____

_____

_____

Date_____

_____

_____

_____

_____

_____

Date_____

_____

_____

_____

_____

_____

Date_____

_____

_____

_____

_____

_____

Date_____

_____

_____

_____

_____

_____

Date_____

_____

_____

_____

_____

_____

Date_____

_____

_____

_____

_____

_____

Date_____

_____

_____

_____

_____

_____

Date_____

_____

_____

_____

_____

_____

I AM SO HAPPY AND GRATEFUL THAT:

_____

_____

_____

_____

_____

_____

_____

_____

_____

_____

_____

_____

_____

_____

_____

_____

_____

_____

_____

Do you have an amazing story you would like to share? To share your own personal story with the world, visit www.BruceGoldwell.com and click on the SUBMIT YOUR STORY link. Use the form on the page to submit your story. If your story is used in one of the *"Mastery of Abundant Living"* books, you will be notified.

Suggested Readings:

Mastery of Abundant Living
Bruce Goldwell and Tammy Lynch

Magical Thinking of the Law of Attraction
Bruce Goldwell, Tammy Lynch and Debbie
Buchanan

New Life Resolutions
Bruce Goldwell, Tammy Lynch and Jean Lauzon

Mission Possible
Carmen J. Day, Steven Covey, Brian Tracy

The NEW Think and Grow Rich
Ted Ciuba

Your Best Life Now
Joel Osteen

The Power of Your Subconscious Mind
Joseph Murphy

Choosing Joy, Creating Abundance:
Practical Tools for Manifesting Your Desires
Ellen Peterson

Printed in the United States
200555BV00003B/70-99/A

9 781897 512012